The Prospect of Redemption

by

Terence F. Moss

To all the lost souls.

For the sins that incarcerate lost souls and for which there is no redemption, they cannot be forgiven. They can only be thankful that they are all just one breath away from freedom and they can fly away...

Other works by the author.

Angels and Kings (Musical)
Sole Traders (Musical)
The Inglish Civil War (TV Comedy)
Closing Time (TV Comedy)
The Killing Plan (Novel)

The Prospect of Redemption

by

Terence F. Moss

Chapter 1

Saturday 9th August 2000. 8am

Today was Sarah's Wedding and while the family's prepared for this long awaited day, Harry laid in his hospital bed, eyes closed, carefully watching the small white dots dancing on his eyelids, wondering whether   he could ever completely evacuate his brain of all the memories that now haunted is soul as easily as his recently failed attempt to exsanguinate his body. If he could, then he might rest easier, but this he could never do, as the recollection was burnt too deep ever to be that easily erased. They were now an integral part of who he was and what he had become.

As the sunlight became a little brighter, he slowly opened his eyes and began to negotiate, with a degree of circumspection that belied his last waking memory, the short journey from a sub-conscious too conscious state. He slowly, methodically, gently rubbed away the sleep dust from the corner of each eye. Now he could clearly see the dismal nature of his reality. He was as unaware of my existence, as I am still a little unsure of it. This was a state of mind that would remain unchanged for many years.

Somewhere in the background, Harry could just hear the mundane ramblings of a hospital radio DJ, which for some reason he found immensely irritating, a plague of insufferable pollution from which there was no escape.

Gazing thoughtfully skywards, the stark reality of his temporary utilitarian surroundings uppermost of which was a shiny white painted ceiling,   should have been evidence enough to anybody that he was obviously still alive. From the ceiling there appeared to be suspended four equally stark, shiny, white painted walls appearing as shivering satin shrouds hanging forlornly down the sides of a very large coffin, each one of approximately equal dimensions. White was the colour, but was it truly a colour he thought, or simply an illusion created by the reflection of intense sunlight? He had begun to question most things these days and those unanswered riddles would come to dominate his brief period of institutional incarceration.

The room appeared clinically clean, which was to be expected. Obsessively tidy with a disturbing element of military precision that he found prosaic and yet strangely intimidating. There was an overwhelming pervasive, almost insidious aroma about it, which was, somewhat annoyingly, slightly reminiscent of a place neither Harry, nor I could immediately remember but which we had both visited at some time in the past.

It had a singular pervasively distinctive smell about it, an unnatural blended ester of disinfectant, Jasmine, eardrops and one other bitter sweet, organic, almost bacterial odour neither of us could clearly identify. Of these fragrances, the Jasmine element brought back pleasurable memories of the garden of a converted farmhouse near the village of Giave in Sardinia that we had rented with a third friend for a the summer nearly twenty years ago. The garden had been allowed to run wild. Wisteria mingled with Jasmine and Rose and was now fighting for domination of ground territory as well as bombarding us with delicate aromatic fragrances in an effort to gain air superiority as well.

It was the height of summer, each day so stiflingly hot and unbearably humid we could do little more than swim the pool, which was permanently at body temperature and not remotely refreshing. When not swimming we would laze in the shade, drink wine and discuss matters of worldly importance and political intrigue, or so we thought at the time, but we were young, innocent and impressionable. Such capricious epitomes of intellectuality were put to one side with the honourable intention they be revisited at some later date, but they never were. Subsequently they, like most idealistic principles, were consigned to be forgotten. Lost in the chronicles of time, as are all dreams when they are inevitably overtaken by the implacable forces of reality and pragmatism in other words, life.

In the evenings, we would slowly amble down the much-travelled gravelly goat path to the nearby village where we would sit for hours eating dinner and getting very drunk in a restaurant perched somewhat precariously high up on the side of a steep mountain.

For obvious reasons, my lasting memory of the holiday was of Nina, the tall raven-haired daughter of Giorgio the owner of the restaurant, she was our waitress each evening. She had large breasts and long strong legs, which I presumed, was normal for a mountain girl, but her most memorable feature was an extraordinary large nose. For some unfathomable reason no one ever mentioned it then, or at any other time after we returned to England. I often wondered in later years, whether it was as bulbous as we had remembered, or whether it had just blossomed in our memories. Its imaginary stature swelling in direct proportion to the increasing number of rejections to our amorous light hearted advances during the holiday. I don't suppose we will ever really know.

I recall an often-told apocryphal story about a simple Mexican farmer who bought a gun to shoot the wild dogs that were worrying his sheep, but ironically and somewhat carelessly he accidently shot the sheep instead due to his extreme short sightedness. After that story had been retold many times and had acquired a few salaciously poetical embellishments on its journey through time, the status of the farmer had been elevated to that of an enigmatic leader of a band of partisan's. The man who shot his own sheep to feed his starving friends and then started a revolution to save Mexico from the oppression of a tyrannical warlord who was starving the people to death. Such is the way with old stories and possibly our only excuse for Nina's blooming proboscis.

I had noticed from past experience, that a man (when in the company of other men) who is constantly rejected by an attractive woman, acquires the dubious ability of being able to produce astonishing statistics, explanations and excuses as to why the rejection was in fact a miraculous escape from a fate worse than death. He will also express his undying gratitude for his deliverance; from what may have been an undesirable end to what was, up to that point in time, a life without a care or responsibility, accountability or reason. All of which he would have had to sacrifice had he been successful in his endeavours.

With such whimsical and bibulously driven conversations, we contentedly passed the hot humid summer nights while being occasionally entertained by Nina, intoning mercilessly about the vagaries and pitfalls of relationships based on an alcohol induced symbiosis. Possibly a warning passed on from her mother - a very religious woman who always dressed head to toe in black, as was the custom - at a very early age and hitherto observed almost obsessively by Nina. She would thereafter probably remain a virgin until it was too late for her to realise that the solicitous virtue, the chaste body and soul that she had so tenaciously protected and withheld as the treasured prize for her betrothed, had now become a dreaded curse.

It was hard to believe, in those long forgotten halcyon days of innocence and naivety what dark demons lay in wait. Like a furniture worm, methodically devouring everything it finds inside the leg of a beautiful chair, only the final barrier of impenetrable varnish prohibiting it from ever leaving the confines of its existence. Until one day on its journey to find fresh wood to devour, it chances upon a small space near a joint, or maybe under the foot where the chair maker had not quite completed his varnishing. From here, it would eventually exit its home leaving behind only the remnants of the leg, now just a fine mixture of regurgitated wood, excrement and detritus encased and supported by a microscopic layer of polish and wood stain. One day, with just a gentle touch the chair would simply collapse into a pile of dust, exposing the years of habitation by an alien lodger who had long since fled the scene. Before that final moment, no one would have been remotely aware of the carnage and destruction being metered out behind the silky thin barrier. The chair that had stood proud for so many years, giving no visible indication that it was slowly being eaten alive from within and like the worm, this demon too was biding its time. Waiting for the perfect opportunity to reappear and begin a journey of purposive destruction that would ultimately strike us all and leave no one completely unscarred or without mortal tarnish.

We spoke then of where we all might be in twenty or thirty years and what would have become of us. Moreover, whether we would even remember these nights. I remember talking at length, as I always did when inebriated, about whether we would all succeed in our chosen professions, or would life not turn out quite as we had expected. Harry once mentioned something we thought a little clichéd even for us pseudo intellectuals; something along the lines of ` *these times were probably the best years of our lives, but we just didn't know it yet and everything else that followed would only see us all looking mournfully back at these days and regretting there passing as something good that we all once had, but which we let slip away.* `

Many years later thinking back to that holiday, I realised how surprising profound and strangely prophetic that statement had been, heavily laden with a grey foreboding almost subliminal subtext, the subtle nature of which neither Charlie, nor I could clearly comprehend or decode at the time. Unusual words for anybody to say when drunk and seventeen, but then for Harry his demons had already arrived long before that day and were now just patiently waiting to reappear and wreak a path of destruction when the time was right.

Before we finally left the island, I believe Harry received a total of seven rejections, which equalled the number of heartfelt pleas for her hand in marriage - this was the record. Charlie and I had only made two offers of marriage each, before deciding to tactfully withdraw from the contest on the basis that Nina might just accept the next offer. Also the fact that we were both appallingly bad gamblers and did not have the requisite facial expressions necessary to successfully bluff it out any further.

Each proposal from Harry had been accompanied with a qualification that he be allowed to sample the goods before effecting the contract. This was a classic example of Harry's innate ability to bluff and obfuscate his real position and intentions, with a masterful degree of cinema verity which could have fooled the gods, well beyond the permissible actuarial limitations of safety and yet still retain a comfortable margin before courting certain and catastrophic disaster.

Once, more in jest then with any realistic expectation of approbation, we did suggest that he might be more successful in his quest, if he were to make a proposal without the condition. Harry however believed with some compelling conviction that Nina would then undoubtedly seriously consider the offer to be too good to reject. His beguiling modesty was truly something to behold. She might even immediately except and as he had, - (and he had clearly stated this on many occasions when the three of us were alone and we had no reason to doubt his integrity) - no desire to throw into turmoil our carefully arranged holiday arrangements, he thought it best to continue as he had done thus far. Happy in the knowledge that should she suddenly become overwhelmed by his intensive and amorous courting ritual and in a moment of weakness concede to his aforesaid intimate proviso, then he could still tactfully and diplomatically, - (and more importantly with Nina's honour, integrity and hymen still perfectly intact in order to obviously forestall any possible repercussions from Giorgio) - withdraw his offer on some quasi-religious, or ethnic incompatibility grounds and nothing would be lost except Nina's hand.

An implausible and inept argument in my opinion, but Harry, as he always did, disagreed. Each rejection therefore statistically and actuarially lessened the odds and increased his and our expectations of a possible successful execution of the marriage contract. The other subject matter of growing concern for Harry however was the appallingly colourful image of domestic humdrum monotony, which we graphically portrayed nightly for him (each demonstration more animated and more depressing than the one before) with Harry and Nina and lots of little Harry's and Nina's being the central protagonists, living a poverty stricken Dickensian nightmare in a rented two bedroom flat over their very own little kebab and chicken shop in Millwall.

The nights were almost as hot, but not so humid as the days due to a cool northerly wind which blew in from the Mediterranean sea most evenings and made eating outside pleasurable, if not sometimes a little tense. We managed to finish our holiday without any agreement on Harry's proposal, but we did make a promise to return the following year with possibly a more interesting and attractive offer for Nina to consider, but we never returned. I often thought of what became of Nina.

Strangely, during the whole of that holiday we slowly became more aware of something that was troubling him, something almost infinitesimal from Harry's distant past, something that precluded him from ever completely letting go. Whatever it was it seemed to reach out and appeared at times to be pulling him back.

Chapter 2

2000. Harry, sitting up in bed and still a little unsure of his precise position in the astral firmament, proceeded to deliberately pinch his left arm with increasing intensity until the pressure became so unbearably grievous, he drew blood. This he reasoned would, to some small degree satiate his assiduous on-going concerns over the suspect reality of his situation. Having satisfied himself beyond reasonable doubt over these concerns, he became immediately aware of the bizarre irony of the sado-masochistic nature of the inflictions and the distinct possibility of the existence of a parallel nihilistic almost existentialistic universe. Having unwittingly delivered himself into this arena he could quite simply have incorporated the arm pinching experience -which was carried out with the precise intention of proving he was actually alive - into some alternative semi-conscious explanation, so that in fact he wasn't where he thought he was after all, but somewhere else altogether. Fortunately, he was not.

He reasoned that he was responsible for his own life and all that happened in it. Nothing was the outcome of some preordained destiny and therefore no sane person would create such an ascetically uninteresting and boring existence to reside in for eternity. Surely if one had a choice, it would be exciting and colourful and all the things you would wish for, but this most definitely was not what he had ever desired.

The early morning summer sun piercing through the half drawn curtains, extinguished any further concerns he may have had, as it haphazardly razored the light crossing the room, like shards of a broken mirror suspended serendipitously in mid-air, each one highlighting the tiny fragments of dust falling from somewhere unknown, this was evidence enough for him. He looked at his watch it was nine forty two, but it took him a little longer to work out what day it was. Harry had only ever visited the cottage hospital once before as a legitimate 'patient' and that was over thirty years ago, when he was seven, to have his arm put in plaster after he had been involved in a road accident. He had collided with an oncoming motor vehicle whilst negotiating a right hand turn off the main road near his boyhood home in Hastings. He had stuck out his left arm and gracefully glided into a right hand turn as if he were an aeroplane banking to the right with one wing raised higher than the other which for some inexplicable reason Harry, who was daydreaming at the time, had unfortunately in a momentary juxtaposition of realism and idealism mistaken for his left arm.

He would think back to this event in years to come and consider carefully whether the forces of evil had militated against him in this contrivance of destiny. Eventually he would arrive at the simple conclusion that there was no malevolent Machiavellian   plot, no hidden agenda underscoring his life and his presupposition of a dark conspiracy was at best extremely doubtful and at worst inspirationally and profoundly delusional.

The manoeuvre although undeniably aesthetically pleasing, elegantly stylish and undoubtedly eloquent in its execution was seriously flawed technically speaking. The ensuing collision; with a green and white 1964 Lotus Cortina GT, which was in immaculate condition before the incident so he was later informed; was being driven by an elderly gentlemen approximate age forty two, who was, somewhat surprisingly - although this did not occur to him at the time, but came back as a recurring nightmare - wearing a light green leather jacket and matching kid leather aerated driving gloves as worn by the legendary Paddy Hopkirk circa 1960. Hopkirk was a hero to all working class lotus Cortina owner-drivers, so I was later informed. The collision sent Harry swiftly and unceremoniously into a more prosaic, untimely and irrefutably unscheduled flight, this one however was graphically illustrated and witnessed by a number of casual bystanders.

Two in particular, were very large women, both in very colourful floral housecoats, hairnets, curlers and pink fluffy slippers as he remembered. However this detail may not have been entirely accurate as he had already (somewhat erroneously) collectively encapsulated all women above the age of twenty-five whom he could remember from this period, including his mother, into this sartorially dismal collective stereotypical image.

This was possibly the first conscious encounter he had experienced with his inadvertent and unintentional predilection as to not so much distort the facts - or obscure the truth with which he was always a little economical - so much as to visually embellish them. An example being the aforementioned two large classic Cookian lady's; this was his artistically enhanced recollection in later years after he had become acquainted with Beryl's work; who were standing only a few yards away at the moment of collision and were at the time intimately engrossed in a heated conversation regarding the apparent demise of popular music since the arrival of the outrageous rebel Cliff Richards, somebody who had supplanted the likes of Al Martino and Elmondo Ross and his Latin American orchestra in popular musical culture. To this day Harry still had a funny déjà vous moment whenever he heard "Hear in my Heart" by Al, playing on the radio.

Harry's eventual reconnection with terra firma was definitely not a dream and ultimately very painful as he landed on his head in the garden of No 38. Fortunately, a very large ornate flowering Fuscia bush broke his fall a lot, his right arm a little, his left fibular a bit, (simple greenstick fracture) and his confidence completely. That, like all the others would eventually recover. Not however the Fuscia bush, which eventually died probably from some form of horticultural anti-falatic shock. His bicycle was severely damaged well beyond economical repair, accordingly to Mr Billington who owned the cycle shop on the corner of Rugmore road and Gladys Avenue.

Harry's awkward gangly landing (no arms or legs where they should have been) produced an alarmingly large bump on his head the size of an egg. The nurses at the hospital who were fascinated by the aberration, proceeded to paint a nose, mouth and two eyes on the bump, much to the amusement of the other inmates and sundry visitors, but to the consternation and interminable chagrin of the consultant Mr Jameson a man of little humour, but unusually gregarious taste in socks as I remember. Today however was different.

Chapter 3

2000. Harry's hospital room had one of those large cast iron radiators under the window. The sort they used to have in Victorian (circa the Great Exhibition) primary schools and on which he used to warm up his pre Thatcher milk in the mid-morning break. The sash window was slightly distorted with age and slightly open at the top. Everything in the room was painted white and was very clean. There were various non-descript pictures hanging on the walls, one of a sandy beach somewhere. Various items of furniture including a side cabinet next to the bed, a small table, two chairs (not matching) another large built-in wardrobe in the corner and what appeared to be some sort of medicine cabinet attached to the wall. There was a basin and cabinet against one wall and as I remember, the tap was dripping. There was one solitary light pendant with a large orange shade hanging from the ceiling and although appearing utilitarian and austere the room emanated a strangely palliative and reassuring aura. This, despite the obvious incongruous presence of twentieth century hi-tech medical monitoring equipment surrounding a bed in a building from another age.

Harry sat up in bed and I noted that both his wrists were bandaged. He was watching something move slowly across the bedroom ceiling, it may have been a spider, or a fly I do not remember. A recording or possibly a radio playing Dinah Washington singing "September in the rain" could just be heard somewhere outside the hospital window, a song I have always loved. Harry was playing with something which I realised was a pencil. He was slowly sliding the pencil, held under pressure between his thumb and forefinger, until his fingers reached the base and then he would allow the pencil to slowly fall back before picking the pencil up from the bottom and repeating the process; each time with more intensity. He stopped for a few seconds, relaxed and wrote something down on a note pad, pondered for a few moments longer on what he had written and then recommenced sliding his fingers down the pencil with ever-increasing pressure while staring at the ceiling. There was a deliberate neurotic intensity to this process as he increased the pressure to the point where his whole body strength appeared to be bearing down on to the tip of the pencil. For a moment, the pencil began to gently shudder, and looked as if it might snap under the immense strain. But it did not. The song ended and somewhere in the distance, church bells began to ring.

There was a knock at the door and before Harry could murmur a word, the door slowly eased opened and she appeared. He instinctively relaxed his tense grip on the pencil, concentrating all his energies and powers of observation on the visage before him, He allowed the pencil to slowly fall through ninety degrees and collapse on the table. She paused for a moment, neatly framed in the doorway before fully entering the room. In those few brief moments of confusion the extreme radiance from the hallway fluorescents cast an angelic mystical aurora around the outer perimeters of her voluminous locks creating a diaphanous and magnificently elegant wraithlike allusion the like of which he had expected one day to experience, but not here and not just yet. Almost in silhouette, she appeared to be holding the staff of life in one hand and the scales of justice in the other. The disturbing majesty of this ethereal image startled Harry. Somewhat puzzled he immediately began to rack his brain as to any obvious reason why, at this particular moment in time he should be bought to account for previous sins, before the grand arbiter of justice on what appeared to be an unscheduled and definitely untimely (as far as he was concerned) final day of judgement, but he could think of only one…

Almost spontaneously and without any direct conscious intervention his fingers stood the pencil firmly upright once again and as the nebulously angelic vision slowly ambled into the room laden down with an assortment of plastic and metal utensils it became abundantly clear that this was not

19

what he had first thought at all, but clearly a visual misunderstanding created by the misrouting of the optical signals to an overactive medial prefrontal cortex. His body was not in fact about to be sequestrated by a greater being for as yet unspecified purposes. The lingering apparition was in fact just a humble ward cleaner holding a mop, bucket and an array of other cleaning implements, which had momentarily created this bazaar almost iconic allusion. Doris, a very large woman of obvious Asian extraction with an exploding cannon ball of black curly hair and a grey cleaner's hat precariously balanced on the top of her head reminded him for reasons he could not readily call to hand, of a statue of a married couple on a wedding cake. Doris, who must have been in her fifties, exuded a prepossessing instantly gregarious disposition as she began slowly casting her eyes around the room as if looking for something in particular, but she was not. Then focusing on Harry who had not taken his eyes off her since she arrived, she smiled disarmingly. Harry could not quite make his mind up whether she had noticed him before or after she had completed her review of the room. This too puzzled him.

Harry smiled back, almost defensively as she dropped the mop and buckets on the floor, each with its own dull, distinctive, metallic clunk. The other items she carefully placed on to the chair.

`Hello love, I'm Doris.` she greeted Harry with a cheery smile and spoke with a strong Jamaican accent with an oddly incongruous, but nevertheless friendly Cockney inflexion...

`Hello Doris,` replied Harry cautiously and with some reservation.

`Alright if I do you now?`

Still a little startled and still recovering from the initial apparition that was now indelibly imprinted in his brain forever, Harry let the pencil drop gently down onto the notepad and nodded approval. He was about to reply when...

`...only Doctors coming round on his rounds,` - she smiled at the alliteration and made some unusual movements

20

with her mouth as if striving to straighten out her lips - `in half an hour and I'm all behind today. ` She bent over to pick up a cloth from one of her buckets and shook her body almost imperceptibly as if someone had just walked over her grave, the vibrations seemed to quiver all the way from head to toe.

`No you carry on,` said Harry. She started to clean the room flicking lightly over the furniture, windowsill and sundry pictures on the wall while humming gently. Oblivious to the fact that she had never met Harry before, she immediately engaged him in conversation, as if they were old friends.

`Got in bloody late this morning, didn't I. My old man forgot to get me up. Not his bleeding fault really, silly old sod can't tell shite from cornflakes since he got his bloody debenture.`

Harry was a little surprised by this disclosure. Although he didn't consider himself to be a snob, he did think that anybody who could afford extortionately overpriced tickets to watch two weeks of Wimbledon tennis would not want his wife, to be working as a lowly paid cleaner in a hospital? This social-eco inconsistency troubled him. Maybe he had jumped to the wrong conclusion he thought, better to venture a response that would engender clarification on the issue rather than make an irredeemable assumption that would see him dammed as an idiot for all eternity.

`Wimbledon! ` said Harry inquisitively, with a tiny hint of hesitancy closely bordering on stunned disbelief.

`Wimbledon, ` replied Doris starkly a little astonished and sounding confused.

`Tennis.` said Harry in clarification, but now becoming a little unsure of his ground, having given some thought to the unusual intonation and inflection of her reply.

`Tennis? Naa he hates bloody tennis. Anyway, his brain's to buggered up for that poncey lark. `

`Dementia! ` Harry suddenly exclaimed with welcome relief as clarity crystallised in his mind and he realised it was nothing more a simple malapropism.

`That's right, that's what I said. You a little deaf? ` Harry shook his head. Doris's expression changed to one of vacuous disbelief.

`My old man's a little deaf these days, especially in the morning. It's his age he'll be sixty-nine in January. `

`I think I just misheard you, ` replied Harry with a sigh of relief.

`Oh.` said Doris who was now not sure whether he too was a little deaf, but possibly in denial, so she smiled back at him, but not in a patronizing way, more the fecund regal pity you would expect from a pious pope politely addressing a stupid peasant. She then carried on cleaning the room and started humming quietly to herself, one of those tuneless oddities that people sometimes hum…

`Don't think I'll bother coming round your place for breakfast though, ` said Harry. Doris stopped cleaning and humming simultaneously and slowly turned to Harry with an expression of deep concern.

`Did they miss you out? They're always doing that in these side wards. The kitchen staff are all bloody foreigners you know, it's an absolute shambles here sometimes and they don't speak a word of English. I'm surprised they can even find this ward...` she paused for a moment to think about what she had just said then continued   `...In fact I'm constantly surprised they can even find the bloody hospital at times.` Harry smiled to himself at the intuitive, if somewhat damming observation, but Doris retained the same calm dispassionate look on her face as before.

`No, No they didn't miss me,` replied Harry effusively, almost apologetically `I was making a joke, a bad one as it appears…`

Doris's expression still didn't change. She turned back and resumed cleaning, but was obviously still thinking deeply about what he had said. After what seemed like a lifetime when one of those awkward moments arises, she stopped again and looked back at Harry with a slight grin. She had obviously come to a conclusion. `Oh I see, shite – cornflakes very funny ha-ha.` Her timing was impeccable, but she still didn't laugh. She just sort of grinned patronisingly with a hint of apprehension as if a little unsure of herself and completely unimpressed by his attempt at casual humour.

`Not in really good taste was it?` said Harry contritely, now feeling very humble and slightly belittled,   as embarrassment slowly swept over his body like a hot flush.

`Not tasty at all if you ask me,` replied Doris looking reproachfully at Harry,   then she suddenly   burst out laughing and the whole room came alive. Harry realised he had been had. This quickly dispelled the previously difficult atmosphere and Doris   continued with the cleaning and resumed   humming contentedly to herself.   Harry acknowledged her clever manipulation of the situation and made a mental note that any further attempts at humorous banter should be very carefully considered before engaging his mouth again, but it still bothered him a little.

`Look, I didn't mean to offend yo.. `

`No.` she interrupted abruptly and shook her head. Her benign expression indicated she had obviously not taken any offence. `It's all right, don't be silly.  Anyway, I could do with a bit of a laugh after the night I've just had with 'im.  It can be a bit grim with the old bugger at times.`

Realising she had not been offended,   any residue of tension he may have felt quickly dissolved. `Can't they do anything for him?  Drugs or something?`

`Na. It's a bit like old Bony and 'es horses.`

`Bonianesorses?` he muttered, gazing up at the ceiling as if praying for divine intervention, he would even settle for earthly   inspiration,   but none was forthcoming as he desperately tried to mentally unscramble the sound he had just experienced. He tried changing the syllable emphasis, but that didn't seem work, then he considered whether it was another mangled malapropism, but nothing sprang to mind. He began to mildly panic and started reflecting on the acute embarrassment he had previously subjected himself too. He was determined, if it were at all possible, to avoid a repeat performance, but he was at a loss. Contemplating further possible humiliation, he looked back at her with a glazed expression petitioning, no pleading for compassion and humanity at this crucial moment of imminent intellectual defeat. She stopped for a few seconds and leaning on her mop in a somewhat precarious manner, realising that he was once again flummoxed, she enunciated the words once more, but much slower;

`Bon-ni-part, Napoleon Bonipart you must remember him?` She emphasized the first `a` as `i` which confused him further.

Not sure he clearly understood where this was going, he cautiously ventured `Emperor of France?`

`That's right Waterloo, Wellington boots, Abba.` Doris replied, blissfully unaware of the tenuous connection.

`Yes I've read about him at school, but I don't remember anything about horses.`

`When they're fucked, ... shoot em. That's what Boni said.`

`Right,............ and that's N.H.S. Policy now is it?` replied Harry, a little taken back by the bluntness of her reply.

`Nooooo don't be silly,` replied Doris admonishingly. `I was just making a point. I just think it's a shame they have to let them linger on. If he was a horse in that condition, Boni would have shot him in the head.` She continued mopping the floor without breaking her rhythm.

`Bit drastic that, isn't it?` asked Harry curiously.

`He's good for sod all else.`

`He must be able to do something?` entreated Harry.

'Not with shit for brains he can't...' replied Doris. Swiftly, closing off that avenue of compassion and consolation.

'Couldn't you put him in a care home or something?' asked Harry.

Doris stopped again and leaned on her mop smiling, 'In a home, na couldn't do that. Love the old bugger too much to stick him in one of those bloody shitholes.'

'You could still visit him every day.'

'What, to see him shitting in bucket or squatting on a piss pot all day with his cacky pants down by his ankles, stinking like a pub urinal? I know all about those homes. Couldn't do that to him. It's very important he retains his dignity, don't yer think?'

Unprepared as Harry was, for this peroration of devotion, loyalty and self-respect, he realised immediately that he had seriously miscalculated and devalued the significance of love and fragility of concern; and the part it played in a personal relationship equation. 'Yes, yes I do,' replied Harry.

'Anyway if I was visiting 'im every day I might as well have him at home where I can keep an eye on 'im, he's no trouble really, been pissing himself for years specially when he gets drunk, so there's nothing new there. He still manages to get to the lavi for twosies most days when I'm not there, so it's not too bad. Have to wipe his arse when I get back from work sometimes and 'is undies can be a right bloody disaster, bit like a monsoon in the Somme. Shit, blood, piss and bullets everywhere, well no bullets actually and not a lot of blood really 'sept when his bum grapes is playing up. Can be a bit of a lark though, sometimes when he's feeling a bit mischievous he hides his doings's and I have to find it.... before we have tea preferably. Found a monster in the bread bin once that made us laugh.'

'Still has a sense of humour then?' asked Harry drolly.

Doris continued mopping the floor. `Oh yes I think you can safely say that and that's my point, he still likes to mess about and make me laugh so he's still there, somewhere and we do have some good times. That's why I couldn't put him in a home, to many happy memories you see. I would miss all that. I can remember the days when he used to make me laugh so much I'd piss me bleeding knickers and then other days he would come home drunk as a lord and give me a right good hiding.`

Harry was a little shocked and surprised at this disclosure. `Did you never think of leaving him?` asked Harry with the naïve innocence of someone who had obviously not fully experienced the trials and tribulations of life and clearly didn't fully understand the intricacies of love, marriage and commitment.

Doris looked at him and pondered over the question for a few moments. There was no hint of dissimulation in her tone, just kind respect and gentle admiration for the man he once was. `No, he loved me really.` she sounded completely surprised and a little taken aback by Harry's suggestion. Were all men such shallow creatures she wondered? There were times when she really did feel as if they were a different species altogether. `He was just having a bad day, don't we all?`

`But he beat you up and you hadn't done anything wrong,` exclaimed Harry still searching for a rational explanation. Not that doing something wrong was any justification for violence, he thought afterwards.

`Sometimes yes, but he didn't mean it really,` replied Doris brushing off the detail as inconsequential and insignificant. `There was no intention to...` but she never finished and left that hanging in the air...

Harry mused over that short declamation, loaded with so much carefully considered loyalty. `I still don't understand why you stayed if he was violent?`

`Don't know why me self really,` replied Doris wistfully. `Ask any woman why she sticks with a bloke who's violent,

...he might be a bastard, but he's my bastard. Least he didn't ignore me, that would be worse.`

`How?` said Harry.

`Indifference that's what ignoring somebody really means, it means you don't even register on their radar, you are there, but they just can't see you. But if they hit you they know you are there, it means your very existence is effecting the way they think, its interrupting their stream of peripheral consciousness, so that has to be good. So no, I couldn't have lived with that, but anything else...` Once again Harry was dumfounded by a prosaic logic he could not fully comprehend or had ever encountered before.

`And so you forgave him.`

`Of course and anyway he stopped all that stuff years ago.`

`So that's why you stayed?...` asked Harry who still seemed to be looking for simple answers to complex questions, when there often wasn't one.

`That and I like sleeping with 'im .. not just the sex and all that lark, well that's all but stopped now anyway, but ....well just being in bed, knowing he's there, feeling the warmth of his body next to mine. Hearing him say "goodnight sweetheart" after we put the lights out, just before we fall asleep. He used to roll over and gently kiss me on my lips or my nose even when he was drunk, that doesn't happen very often now.` Her voice tailed off a little and was almost inaudible. She must have been thinking about different times...

`I know he farts like an elephant and snores like a pig, but that don't matter really it's... I suppose it's comfortable, almost reassuring in a funny sort of way and you feel secure just for a few hours when it's just the two of you alone in bed all cuddled up, like. I don't suppose any woman can really explain it, least not until their man's gone. Then it all seems so clear that they can't think why they put up with it in the first place. Might be love I don't know. Maybe when you live with a bloke your brain goes a bit soft, then again we all think we can change a bloke into something different, so maybe we stay... `cause we're too stubborn to leave and admit defeat. I stayed with him and he did change a little bit, eventually. But it's all different now. I mean he's all I got in 'e and I do love the old sod.`

`Sounds like he brought you a lot of love and happiness?` asked Harry.

`And some heartache but then they go together, don't they. You can't have one without the other that's the rule.` replied Doris thoughtfully.

`The rule.` asked Harry curiously.

`The Rule of life.` replied Doris. `If you want love, you have to give love and if you give love you are going to get some heartache in return one day and that's the simple truth of the matter, but then that's why we're here, so if you don't love - it all means nothing.`

`Been some heartache then?` asked Harry thinking back to his own past..

`And a lot of joy that's why I love him. Mind you, he does try me patience at times when 'e pisses on me rhubarb. But it don't matter what happens really 'cause, we still got each other, that's all that matters As long as we're alive we'll keep bashing on together holding hands till the day we pop our clogs, cause that's all we got left now, that and the memories. There ain't nothing else and there definitely ain't no reruns, this is it. So you just have to hang on and see it out to the bitter end, haven't yer?` Doris started mopping again.

`You're beginning to makes me feel a bit.. `

`Of a twatt?` Interrupted Doris. Harry was a little surprised by this seemingly unwarranted, unexpected insult.

`Twat? No, I wasn't going to say that I was going to say humble actually.` said Harry indignantly.

`Humble? Naa, you're not humble, you're a twatt. You might be feeling a bit humble right now, but you're still a twat and a useless one at that if you ask me. You're the one who tried to do yourself in aren't you?

`Sort of...` replied Harry cautiously, now acutely aware that the topic of conversation had suddenly been diverted down a dark side road and across a very muddy field.

`Sort of? No sort of about it. Bloody stupid thing to do in the first place if you don't mind me saying - especially as you buggered it up an all - which probably means you didn't have your heart in it anyway. I mean how hard is to cut your bleeding wrists, it's not, it's easy. That's how hard it is. That's why I think you're a bit of a twatt. It's all been a bit of a self-indulgent whinny for attention and a complete waste of time if you ask me. What with using up valuable hospital resources when we're stretched to the limit as it is with financial cutbacks and central resourcing and here we are wasting our precious time on somebody who ain't really sick except maybe a bit in the head...`

Harry was beginning to wonder whether the human resources management had, inadvisably, under the pressure of fiscal restraint, decided to amalgamate the hospital's psychiatric analysis unit and hygiene department into a sort of all-encompassing physosantitation division. It was beginning to seem that way.

`You don't know anything about me. So I don't know how you can say that,' replied Harry sounding a bit flustered. He paused for a few moments while he gathered all his faculties back together.

'I am not a twatt and I am definitely not "*sick in the head*" as you so quaintly put it,' continued Harry with a retort of challenging intensity that clearly and without any ambiguity clearly demonstrated how incensed he was by Doris's blunt clinical assessment of his state of mind. Being also a little unsure of her real qualifications and slightly disturbed by her unprofessional sounding diagnosis he also wondered whether this might be a possible clue to her real intentions. He surmised that maybe while operating under the modus operandi of benign hospital cleaner, she was covertly engendered to quickly assess his true mental state and clean his bedroom at the same time. A sort of all in one clean room - check brain project.

Doris stopped for a moment, leaned on her mop and thoughtfully considered his reply. `Yes you are. Look, what are you thirty-five, prime of life, bet you got nothing wrong with you except for a big dollop of self-pity and you want to go and end your life. Bet you're going to upset a lot of people when you do, do it, specially your mum. She will be heartbroken. Had you thought about that? She's the one that will suffer most. She's the one who brought you into this world wiped your arse and probably looked after you every single day till you was able to look after yourself which was probably last Thursday by the looks of things. You're part of her and if you kill yourself, you will kill part of her, a big part of her, had you thought of that?`

`No but...,` Harry was now certain he had been surreptitiously co-opted into an as yet unnamed hospital finance initiative. Paranoia played a not insignificant part in his thoughts these days.

`Nope thought not,` interrupted Doris. `Self, self, self, that's all you young ones ever think about. Look at me and my old man, both knackered, Christ it's all I can do to peddle home on me bike sometimes, but we struggle on.` Doris sighed...

Harry thought about that for a moment and his brain began to conjure up a strange Hieronymus Bosch type image of Doris on her bike, which was being partially consumed by her ample posterior. With buckets hanging off the handles bars and brushes and mops tucked under her arms while cycling up a road with her husband chasing after her with his underpants in one hand and a bunch of Rhubarb in the other. It was going to take some time for him to completely eradicate this image from his mind.

`But you won't see me knocking it on the head without a fight, just because I got a bit of a drip on; and we haven't got any children we could love, so heavens knows we've got a right to feel  pissed off with how life's treated us, but we aren't.`

`You haven't any children?' said Harry `So how come you know so much about a mother's loss if you've never had any. Not exactly speaking from experience are you?` He realised almost immediately how crass and insensitive that sounded.

`Didn't say we didn't have any, what I actually said was we haven't got any. We did have a little girl in fact, but she died before she was a year old, then we had a boy and he died just before he was two. Some sort of blood disorder - hereditary I was told - on my side, so we decided we couldn't go through that again and...` Doris paused for a few seconds and drifted off somewhere, where maybe sad endings are different or maybe they don't even happen.

`Broke Charlie's heart it did. He never said anything, never mentioned it not once ever. Never blamed me, but you could see the sadness in his face. Something left him after they died and it never came back. Charlie always wanted a son just so he could play football with him and go fishing and all the other things that dads do when a son is growing up. In addition, he wanted a daughter so he could see her all dressed up, looking beautiful on her wedding day and he could walk her down the aisle, the proudest man in town. He was really looking forward to that, it meant so much to him and he was so happy when they were born and when it didn't happen well....`

`I am sorry,  I shouldn't have said what I said.`   said Harry.

`It's not your fault nothing to apologise for, you didn't know, it just that at times like this I see people like you and I think back to all the things we had hoped for and all the dreams we had and they all came to nothing... oh what I'd give to be as young as you again. All the things I wanted to do, places I wanted to go, but never had the chance, I could have done them once, but I won't do them now it's too late now, we're . . . too old.'

31

'Too old! Too old for what?' asked Harry almost reproaching her for using age as an excuse not to fulfil dreams.

'Everything,' replied Doris sadly.

'Like what?' enquired Harry encouragingly her with his optimism, 'give me a for instance?'

Doris stopped what she was doing, shut her eyes and thought about the question for a moment. 'Cuba.' she announced. Her eyes now wide open again and shining mischievously.

'Cuba?' repeated Harry quizzically, not sure whether he had misheard her again.

'I always wanted to go to Cuba. Read lots of books about it. Do you know they train some of the best doctors in the world? We even have one here in this hospital, '...and he speaks English.' There was a disturbing element of surprise in her voice while imparting that little vignette of acerbity.

'Castro done all that, so he can't be all bad. Might keep his people destitute, but they're very healthy and happy.' Harry could see a certain irony in that statement that seemed to have completely passed Doris by. She obviously held the dictator in high esteem. 'Have you ever been there?' she asked

Harry looked at Doris and smiled. She had obviously read some pro Castro propaganda in a Sunday supplement and naively believed it. 'Went to Havana once a few years ago,' said Harry.

'Havana?' enquired Doris thoughtfully.

'It's in Cuba,' added Harry.

'Yes I know that.' she replied with a wry smile.

'I loved it,' said Harry.

'There you are see, already been to places that I wanted to visit, but never will. What was it like?'

'Very hot, very quiet and strangely uncomplicated,' replied Harry in a whispered tone. Remembering this long

32

forgotten memory had a calming effect on Harry's previously slightly strained almost guarded manner. Even the tension in his fingers slowly melted away for a while. Up to now all conversation had bordered on somewhere between melancholic disinterest and painful recollections, but the mention of Cuba induced a palliative dimension, which seemed to emanate from somewhere deep within his soul.

`Uncomplicated?` enquired Doris.

`Yes not like here where everything is connected to something, but for most of the time you don't really know to what. I suppose that's why most people really go on holiday just to get away from all the complications of normal everyday life, but it's only an illusion, you never really escape reality. You can run away and hide from it for a while, but it has a nasty habit of catching up eventually. But it did feel different out there, good, for a while.`

`It sounds lovely,` said Doris embracing the thought. `I used to have a dream I was dancing the Samba all night in some shady nightclub in South America with me Charlie. He was a lovely dancer once, a long time ago now, when we was courting... that would have been nice. I saw Richard Gere do it in a film once. I thought it was so romantic just like me and Charlie used to be. All candles and things like that. A sultry muggy atmosphere, lots of cigar smoke swirling around, men with black Fedora's and the heavy aroma of dark rum and sweat, lovely.` For a moment Doris drifted off in a daydream again to another world, another existence. This one a little better than the last one she visited.

`Did you go dancing when you were there?` asked Doris wistfully after a few moments.

`I did once, in a very hot nightclub in Havana,` replied Harry. `It's not like dancing over here, it is different, it's.... it's more like making passionate love, but with your clothes on.`

Doris felt a little uneasy at the candid nature of his explanation, but then realised that of course he was right. Latin American dancing was all about the passion and intimacy. It always promised to lead to somewhere and it would always take you to a place where you could forget the whole of the world and all the bad things in it. You could just lose yourself for a while. That is what he had managed to do while he was there. For a few brief days, he had forgotten nearly everything that haunted him. His demons couldn't find him there.

`You know what they say, Love like you have never loved before, sing like no one can hear you and dance as if no one can see you and I did. You lose all your inhibitions out there nobody cares. You should go, just once,` implored Harry.

`I always wanted to,` replied Doris, `but not now, it's too late for us. But you could go again, you could do anything at your age. That's why I think you're selfish. Life's just too precious to throw it away for nothing.`

`It's my life,` exclaimed Harry indignantly. Gone was the languid atmosphere of their previous words.

`Yea, your life,` replied Doris, `but there's a bloody idiot in charge of it. You could be back there, dancing every night instead of hanging around here waiting to die.`

`I'm not waiting to die,` said Harry strongly refuting her allegation.

`Aren't you?` replied Doris sternly, looking him squarely in the face, his expression didn't change and neither did Doris's, but they both knew he was lying.

Harry smiled at Doris. `I think you have to be in love to dance the samba properly. I can see you still are. You should take your Charlie.`

`I couldn't take Charlie to Cuba, I can't take him to Tesco's without some bloody disaster happening, so I'd hate to think what he'd get up to on a plane.`

`You could go on your own if you wanted to...` suggested Harry cautiously.

`Me?` exclaimed Doris with surprise, `On me own - to Cuba - without me Charlie to protect me - with all those

Latin lovers groping my arse, no I don't think so. Don't know what might happen. Anyway, I'd be lost without Charlie, I couldn't live without him now. We've been together for so long. I wouldn't enjoy life without him anymore.`

`So you still enjoy life then?` asked Harry.

`.. cause I do. I love getting back home each day and sitting down with a nice cup of tea with Charlie. Put the telly on, put me aching feet up for half an hour, its lovely.`

Harry looked at Doris without saying anything while he thought about what she had said.

`So would you kill yourself if you had to carry on without him?` asked Harry ingenuously.

Doris stopped dusting and turned to look at him, a little surprised by the bluntness of his question. She wasn't one to ever mince her words, definitely didn't suffer fools gladly. Working in a hospital, she had become accustomed to the recurring mortal attrition and the daily expunging of life, but the directness and personal dimension of the question caught her off guard. She had thought about it many times, but had never told anybody that she had thought about it; and she had never considered actually discussing it with anyone, as it would not seem to serve any purpose. It was for this reason that she was unsettled by Harry's apparent depth of introspection into arenas she would never normally visit and this was being conducted by someone she hardly knew. This was an unnerving and unexpected twist, which stretched the boundaries of the natural dynamic of their brief relationship. It demanded an element of measured bravado and a dispassionate detachment that would be sufficient to deflect any further incursion into the issue. `Would I do myself in if he died? She repeated, `What sort of a question is that, Noooo, don't be so bloody stupid.`

`But you said you wouldn't live without him.` replied Harry who was not giving up that easily and pressed the point a little further in anticipation of a favourable outcome which could too some small degree ameliorate his own guilt by some sort of mutual indemnification.

`There you go again,` replied Doris politely, `muddling up your words. I said couldn't live without him, not wouldn't and it's very important you use the right one, because they do mean something slightly different.`

`So not that lost then?` asked Harry.

`Yes I would be lost, but not suicidal. You just can't go topping yourself because you're grieving, I could get over it,` she smiled at Harry `and I would get over it.`

`I see.` said Harry contemplatively, becoming acutely aware that her worldly wise answers were not such spur of the moment spontaneous replies as they first appeared to be. He had committed the cardinal sin of seriously under estimating Doris's latent intellectual capacity and he was paying dearly for this woeful lapse in attention.

`If we all stuck our heads in the oven whenever we were grieving then we'd be six deep in bodies by teatime.` replied Doris smiling drolly at Harry.

`Hypothetically then?` replied Harry, `if you were really lonely and missing Charlie would you?` Harry was being tiresomely persistent on this point, but was also painfully aware of the need to shut down any possible avenues of ambiguity which she would undoubtedly exploit in furtherance of her argument.

`Hypothetically speaking,` replied Doris carefully thinking this out as she went `I suppose I might, but not in the half-hearted way you tried. If I was going to do it, I think I'd blow my head off with Charlie's shotgun. He still keeps it loaded under the bed just in case.

`In case?` enquired Harry curiously, `in case of what?`

`We get burgled and he has to protect my...` Doris paused for a moment searching for the right word and having found it smiled serenely at Harry `Virtue.`

Harry smiled back curiously `Your virtue?` he muttered inquisitively not certain what precisely she was referring to, even briefly considering the remote possibility that she might just be the owner of some hitherto unknown and as yet undiscovered priceless religious icon of the same name. On balance he realised this was a highly unlikely probability. Any further confusion he may have had was quickly put to rest when Doris proceeded to point somewhat coyly to the lower area of her abdomen, thereby immediately extinguishing any remaining ambiguity.

'That's what me Charlie likes to call it,' added Doris.

'Oh.' said Harry feeling a small wave of embarrassment wash over him.

'Mind you if a burglar stumbled across us in the middle of the night and we was at it, me in me curlers and bed socks being straddled by 'im with no teeth, a big airy arse sticking up in the air, sweating like a pig, banging his little heart out like a gooden and what with his wind problems and all - they'd probably die of shock anyway. Hate to think what any bystanders might make of it, not that we ever did anything like that you understand,' which she added as an afterthought before suddenly realising that she had unintentionally alluded to the possible presence of an audience to their lovemaking, which of course was definitely not the case. Doris, now more than a little embarrassed by the vision she had accidentally and inadvertently conjured up, wasn't quite sure how she had arrived at this moment of intimate disclosure and with someone, she had only just met. But then isn't that the way of the world that we discuss with complete strangers something we would never consider sharing with a lifelong friend. Maybe there is something about the total absence of an emotional dimension in a relationship, which embraces the sensation of a harmless and benign objectivity when sharing the same information with a stranger.

'A definite case of frightening the horses without any doubt,' she mumbled almost incoherently to herself. Harry smiled to himself at the self-deprecating honesty she had displayed once again, but his face showed little sign of it.

There was silence for a few seconds as they both digested their thoughts and what thoughts they must have been.

`You still... do it` asked Harry almost incredulously, `what with his problems and all...?` He was even more than a little surprised at the indelicacy of a question that had clearly emanated - no escaped was probably nearer the truth - from his own mouth without him even being aware he had said it. A definite case of mouth operating before brain had been properly engaged again.

He knew he should have stopped there, but curiosity, the seriously underrated arbiter of all whimsical knowledge, gossip, tittle tattle, innuendo, supposition careless whispers and rumour had got the better of him again, he should have remembered the cat's problem with it.

`Of cause we do. A woman's got needs you know and a man get urges. He's not always completely do dally tat,` replied Doris demurely with commendable chivalry. `He still has his moments,` she added after a few seconds.

`Do dally tat?` mused Harry to himself, an interesting colloquialism derived from butchery back slang he believed, a long lost language of the meat trade from the early twentieth century. Harry paused again now wondering how to politely extricate himself from this tawdry conversation, but found it impossible to negotiate any kind of meaningful exit without causing offence, so he continued to engage with Doris and hoped for the best.

`Sounds very messy,` Harry muttered cautiously. No that was a mistake he thought. Should have made a specific reference and not left it too vague, but it was too late, the horse had galloped away from the stable.

`No it's not too bad.` replied Doris solicitously, while gazing contentedly into the air with an air of wistfulness that belied the true gravity of such an occasion. `I have a plastic cover on the bed under the sheet in case of emergencies. Nothing gets through that and I'm used to a bit of shite.` Harry winced painfully, but not so that Doris would notice, as the mental imagery played across his brain in full colour widescreen 3D. Not since the films of Sam Peckinpah late of Fresno, had he encountered such visceral carnage.

`I meant the shotgun bit,` replied Harry apologetically pointing two fingers shaped like a gun at his head and pretending to blow his brains out.

`Oh! No, sorry I thought we was still talking about...` she stopped and made a pelvic jerking gesture pertaining to intercourse,

`No not worried about that. I ain't got to clear it up. That's the council's job to scrape me brains off the wall and I won't have to pay for it either. The main thing is its quick and there would be none of yer lingering goodbyes. I can't be doing with all that 'Love Story' twaddle. If you're goner die for fuck's sake get on with it and stop pissing around that's what I think.

`Right,` replied Harry yet again taken aback by Doris's blunt pragmatism.

`So as I was saying you buggered up what was a very easy little number, so I don't really think your heart was in it, just looking for a bit of tea and sympathy if you ask me, all a bit silly really wasn't it?` She looked patronisingly at Harry.

`You think so?` He replied, continually being surprised by the simple lucidity of Doris's burgeoning perception.

I had always thought it's what we do and what we say that defines who we really are. If you say nothing for fear of rebuke or ignominy, you concede to sycophancy, or worse still obsequiousness. The overriding memory you leave behind for others to recall long after the moments of clarity and wise council are forgotten, is that of indifference and apathy and for that, you will be eternally despised or just simply forgotten. I don't know which is worse.

If you create something be it whimsical or tangible then the evidence will always exist and be there to defend your motives (whatever they may be) your reason and your contemporaneous thoughts long after you have been returned to the earth. It will be for others to discuss the quality, integrity and worth of what you have done. Whether it is good or bad is inconsequential for the final evaluation will always be made by other more robust authorities and the quality of those will be governed by the content of your creation. Over that, you have no dominion. Maybe suicide could be a work of art. The delicate balance of any relationship can twist and turn on just a few badly chosen words, or an unintentional gesture... these were and on reflection must have effected Harry's judgement.

`Tell me something.` said Doris quizzically... `What is it that's makes someone want to take their life?` The delivery lacked the synthetic empathy and distilled passion of skilled therapy, but this was adequately compensated for, by a directness that engendered, even demanded a reply of equal integrity.

`One.` replied Harry, but then he thought for a few moments and corrected himself.

`No two reasons. The first is you can't see a significant reason to bother going on after you have accomplished everything you think you will ever be able to do. You have finally arrived at that moment when you have to accept that there are many things you wanted to do that you will never be able to, because you just don't have the ability. That is the moment when there is no point in hanging around any longer as there is nothing left to fill your life and every day just becomes another pointless rerun of yesterday.`

`But surely we all have the ability to do whatever we want to do, whatever we want to turn our hand to if we really want.` replied Doris with a naïve innocence that belied her previous incisive perception.

`No we don't, that's the point,` said Harry enthusiastically. `We may think we do, but if we are really honest with ourselves and that is the one person you should be totally honest with, we don't. Not everybody is good at something, some people just aren't good at anything and the older you get the more honest you become with yourself and the more you realise there is no such thing as infinity or immortality. Everything has a natural lifespan and does eventually come to an end, but sometimes it just takes a little longer than it should. Secondly, you want to do one last thing, make one final statement. A declaration that you still have the ability to do something inspired, spontaneous, something that will have an effect on everybody, makes them think that it all was worthwhile, something that actually makes them realise that you did exist even if you have kill yourself to prove it. Perversely you will never see the effect your final proclamation has on everybody, but if you could wouldn't that be perfect? The ultimate sacrifice for the definitive reaction. You see it's all to do with primary motivations. We need constant reassurance, recognition of our existence. It's the applause of a satisfied audience, the pat on the back for a job well done, the smile and the kiss from a wife when you return home that makes you feel wanted needed, the ....` Harry paused for a moment and looked down at the pencil he was playing with.... `.. we are all addicted performers, all actors and we constantly crave the exhilarating chill of the golden opiate, euphorically spiralling through our veins and around our brains lifting us up once more from our ordinary existence, but the hit dulls the senses and extinguishes reality and one day it doesn't work anymore and you can't hide any longer. You have to face up to the truth and that's what I did.` He looked up at Doris with a pained expression of penitential contempt and asked... `Can you see that? `

`And what was the truth?` asked Doris in a reverential compassionate tone more befitting a priest at confession than a hospital cleaner.

`I've did something wrong,` replied Harry a little sharply, deep within a thought that was obviously troubling him.

`Haven't we all,` mumbled Doris. But not with an air of retrospective agreement, more the tone of casual philosophical acceptance having now resumed her cleaning activities and endeavouring to finish moping under Harry's bed.

`No! Something terribly wrong,` repeated Harry, slightly louder than before and with exaggerated clarification.

`Well I ain't heard anything about it,` replied Doris quietly, not heeding too much attention to the elevated tone (she had had plenty of experience of this in this in the past and knew how best to deal with it) choosing to lessen the heightened tension evident in Harry's voice by maintaining a perfectly balanced almost monotonic pitch.

`It was a long time ago, ...nearly thirty years, nobody knows.` Harry had responded almost immediately to Doris's soporific manner and became quieter and less abrasive.

`Took yer time confessing?` asked Doris inquisitively, still continuing to clean as she spoke.

`I didn't know it was wrong when I did it, I only know now that it was wrong,` replied Harry with a sense of tacit acceptance of the inevitable. Doris stopped for a moment and leaned on her mop.

`My ole man used to say that after 'e hit me, I always found that very reassuring while I was crawling round the floor looking for me teeth.` There was a peculiar element of contradiction to this statement that confused Harry. He looked at her teeth, they looked fine to him and yet the simple honesty of words seemed to refute the obvious evidence before him. She could of course have been wearing dentures, but they didn't look that good, therefore he had to presume that she did in fact have all her own teeth and she was simply using this as an interesting metaphor, but for what he pondered... maybe, it indicated that she too had historical issues that had never been fully resolved.

`Do you think that makes a difference?` asked Harry cautiously.

`What having teeth?' replied Doris abruptly. `Definitely.` she smiled. Her teeth did look good...

Harry ignored the inane flippancy as he was now beginning to understand how Doris's mind worked.

`Not knowing,` said Harry, for the purpose of clarification.

`What!` declared Doris. `You mean if you didn't know what you did, was wrong when you did it, was it wrong? She said this with just a tiny hint of scepticism and incredulity.

`Yes!` responded Harry, realising that the apparently non-invasive nature of her conversational manner was clearly designed to subtly and unobtrusively extract further information without actually asking a direct question. He had concluded many years ago that maybe this was why female detectives were more effective at extracting information from men, than men were. The male of the species is, in the main naturally evasive, vague, ambiguous, precocious and inherently designed, and inclined to be a pathological liar and these traits were serious flaws, but above all else they were arrogant, which was something that could easily be exploited by a woman's unassuming guile.

He was of the opinion that almost any woman of reasonable intelligence had a natural capacity for interrogation, which was the equal of, if not manifestly superior to, any legally trained inquisitor. This predatory and naturally instinctive behavioural ability enabled them to focus on and drill down to the smallest inconsistency in any incomplete, or contentious logic. Once a chink in the armour had been detected, they were then capable of extrapolating tangentially, this speck of information into either a robust defence of their viewpoint, or the destruction of a long held narrative.

Their pre-programmed ability to remember the most insignificant detail which could and often would, be recalled at will, years after an event, gave them an unassailable psychological advantage. Fortunately this unique ability was utilized sparingly and only under the most severe conditions, but nearly always with devastating effect. This almost maternal and deliberately honest approach at interrogation surreptitiously crept under the male defence mechanism, which invariably kicked in immediately another alpha male was introduced into the equation.

`Don't know,` said Doris. `…Don't know what it was you did do I? Anyway, you said nobody knew and if nobody new, maybe it wasn't wrong after all. I mean, how can it be, if no one knows you did it. There has to be somebody to say it is wrong, for it to be wrong. Bit like a fart in the jungle. If no one hears it except you, was it really a fart?` It was a ridiculous analogy and she was obviously paraphrasing small elements of the chaos theory, which she must have picked up from some hospital magazine or newspaper and was now putting her own interesting idealistic take on it.

`I didn't know when I did it.   I just know it now.` reiterated Harry.

`Are you sure you're not making something out of nothing love?` asked Doris. `The mind can play funny tricks. I still remember a lovely old Jewish lady I used to do for years ago told me something I have never forgotten. She had some lovely silver candlesticks and a little grey beard that came to point, (she gestured). Looked a bit like Fagin come to think of it.' *The   stereotypical anti-sematic caricaturisation seemed to have gone straight over her head, Dickens had a lot to answer for.* Anyway, she was always happy and smiling despite all the things that had happened to her and her family and she'd had some terrible things happen to her in the past I can tell you. I remember she was all electric, wouldn't have gas in the apartment. Anyway, I asked her one day how come she was always so happy with life with all that had happened to her and she told me what her secret was. `Life is basically very simple,` she said. `Its people that bugger it up and they do that by thinking too much about what they want and how they are going to get it and that is when it becomes  complicated and when things get complicated people become  frustrated and that's makes them unhappy so just be happy with what you have.`

Doris delivered this homily with a very bad cockney Jamaican Jewish accent for extra effect.

'Isn't that what you're doing, thinking too much? ' Doris asked.

'Maybe,' replied Harry contemplatively. He agreed totally, but he was not going to admit that to Doris.

'Keep it simple, very simple,' added Doris summarising her advice. 'Don't think too much and you'll be ok.'

Harry, thought about what she had said, but was still undecided as to whether the compliant nature of the parties in a relationship was conducive or ultimately inwardly destructive. Surely, its continuance must depend to some degree on a confrontational dimension to the alliance, one that left the door open for discussion and debate and constantly challenged its parameters and boundaries in order to establish precisely where they were. You cannot know the strength of anything until you have tested it to destruction; the trick is to know when to stop before that happens.

'I think about the truth and that must make a difference,' said Harry defensively.

'Think about it by all means,' Doris replied, 'but then put those thoughts away in a box and forget about them that's what I say, but then I ain't a doctor I'm just a cleaner. So what do I know?' she smiled at Harry and Harry stared back at her searching for a gap in the smokescreen she had created.

'Let me give you one other small piece of advice for what it's worth, it doesn't matter how bad your life might seem right now, it's still a whole lot better than no life at all... and there's plenty in the graveyard that would love to swap places with you no matter how bad it might be.'

'I'd swap right now,' said Harry without a moment's thought or indecision.

'What?' replied Doris a little surprised, 'You'd rather be rotting in the ground being eaten by worms, than sitting in bed having this cosy little chat?'

'I'd escape from what is in my head.' replied Harry. He'd often thought about the ritual parody of death. The whole theatricality of the last performance, the final curtain, the fond fair well, but was this all not some elaborate rort merely to service the pockets of funeral directors? He had a cynical opinion of most people, things and occupations and undertakers were not to be excluded. The charade of flowers especially at gravestones had always confused and disturbed him for the recipient never saw them and in most cases would be residing permanently where they would be growing quite freely in all senses of the word for the foreseeable future anyway and the donor would see them only briefly. So hardly anybody would derive long-term enjoyment from them except the owner of flower shop, who obviously benefited financially from the transaction and any occasional passing gravestone reader with a horticultural interest. However, these were surprisingly rare in his limited experience.

The irony of life increasingly annoyed him. With each passing year, he had come to realise that the longer it took to completely understand its complex nature, the less time he had left to actually enjoy it. Ipso facto in a world of perfect symmetry, the precise moment you achieved absolute clarity and enlightenment would undoubtedly coincide with exact moment you fell off the perch.

`Escape yes,` asked Doris curiously, `but where to?`

`I don't know maybe Valhalla.`

`Valhalla,` repeated Doris with a measured insouciance. She had learnt over the years not to take anything too seriously, even death.

Harry thought about what he just said and smiled to himself. `I suppose anything is better than this. Anyway, I am not going to be buried in the ground that's for certain. I would rather have a Viking funeral on the lake.` There was an obvious whimsical dimension to this statement which further amused him.

`I think you'll probably have to settle for the crematorium,` replied Doris more prosaically. `You don't look the slightest bit Scandinavian. Could also be bit of a problem with the council, having a flaming cortège drifting haphazardly around the lake causing untold carnage to the day-trippers out in their pedalo's.`

`Could be quite an attraction,` suggested Harry, but without any real conviction. Tiring of this bazaar conversation Doris thought it was a good time to make her exit. `I can't stand around all day nattering about the meaning of life, I've got another three wards to do, but you remember what I said and you have a think about it, but not too long though hey?` Doris gathered up her mop and bucket and sundry other cleaning tools and made towards the door.

`Oh and one more thing...` she added, glancing back at Harry.

`What?` replied Harry reluctantly adopting a more serious tone as he was half expecting another depressing reality check or hackneyed homily?

`Promise me you'll go back,`

`Back?` repeated Harry a little confused.

`To Cuba,`

`Cuba,` replied Harry still sounding a little confused before everything suddenly fell into place. He grinned at Doris. `Yes I promise, I'll go back,` he thought he might as well play this out to the end, `...and dance the Samba just for you.`

`That would be good,` replied Doris, `Thank you.`

` See yer, tomorrow... for breakfast,` asked Harry.

Doris smiled, `Cornflakes?` Harry puts his earphones back on and Doris closed the door and left Harry's life.

If I had the choice, I would rather have been rich and lived in the 1930's thought Doris walking up the hallway towards the next ward, but it was just a passing thought.

Chapter 4
1990.

David Marshall cautiously entered the main bar of The End of the Bridge Tavern with good reason, for this was no simple drinking house. A more aptly named establishment and gathering point would be hard to find to describe a place where the rejects and intractable combatants ostracised from society congregated to militate with others who had been conspired against - as they in turn prepared to wage their daily encounter with government bureaucracy. This was the umbilical cord through which the detritus and sustenance of physical existence entered and exited, moving garrulously from depressing reality to the infinity of purgatory.

On passing through the door you were immediately assailed by a profound sense of a loss of humanity, a feeling of hopelessness quickly overwhelmed other senses, as you became aware that the last vestige of civilisation had been left behind and that you were now entering the kingdom of despair. The pervasive sadness permeating every darkened crevice gave it the bleak finality of a repository for dying souls immersed in a torpid well of remorse.

The building had obviously been seriously neglected by whoever the owners were, probably through deliberate intent rather than simple obliviousness and had not been redecorated for some considerable time. Despite disparate evidence of the occasional perfunctory, pedestrian attempts at cosmetic refurbishment by various itinerant journeyman landlords - each of whom probably had their only story to tell as to how they had washed up on this particular shore - the badly stained wall paper covered with an eclectic array of dried body fluids, secretions and other unidentified matter was evidence enough of a total disinterest in the moral and physiological management of the establishment.

The decor would probably cause grave health concerns if ever professionally analysed. Cigarette smoke stained all surfaces and fittings and the colourless carpet - no not colourless, for there was some evidence that it was in fact once an attractive floral design, but was now a dark brown and emanated the irredeemably sour stench of stale beer and fresh vomit. However, for all this, the earthy atmospheric attraction was undeniable. David had been here many times before over the years, but that did little to assuage the pervading sense of menace and malevolence he felt tonight, for that was always present and today was no exception. He slowly edged his way across the noisy bar to where Ashley was sipping the final dregs of his pint while leaning languidly against the bar watching a growing crowd of customers who were huddled together in the centre of the room jeering at something. The background music was loud and conversation was inhibited by this and the additional uproar of the heckling crowd, a noise that seemed to be growing in intensity.

`What's happening Ash?` asked David struggling to be heard over the noise.

`Davy boy, how are you love?` Ashley Brakespeare spoke with the fading eloquence and reverential remnants of a public school accent and although his turn of phrase initially gave the impression of overt affection, it was in fact a completely benign corruption of conventional syntax and bore no specific relationship to gay colloquialism or any other form of conventional affection. It could almost be considered to be an address of disaffection under the right circumstances. He looked a little out of place in this woefully neglected sink estate hostelry, a situation to which he was now resigned. Fate had dealt him a miserable hand when it had lifted him up unceremoniously from the glorious spires and academia of Oxford and deposited him here in Hayleigh Downs, but that was another story.

`I'm... fine,` replied David carefully accentuating each word. `What - is - going - on?`

`Would you like a drink?` mumbled Ashley who was obviously a little drunk and oddly distracted by the commotion in the centre of the room. He appeared to be completely unaware of the level of noise, which was drowning out all normal conversation and continued to speak without raising his voice. David was a little confused by this, as it seemed to defy physical logic. He even considered just for a moment, whether he too should adopt a less sonorous tone, but quickly discounted that as completely impractical.

`In a minute mate,` replied David. `What's all that racket about?` nodding his head in the direction of the crowd.

`Malci has returned,` replied Ashley with a foreboding, disconsolate air that spoke volumes about something.

`Who?` replied David who didn't quite catch the name and had to raise his voice as he was still having trouble understanding what Ashley was saying and was now becoming distracted by the swelling crowd.

`Malci, Malci Shaw,` replied Ashley. There was a tiny detectable element of consternation perforated with a trace of despondency in his voice that was clearly tangible despite his inebriated condition.

`I thought he was banged up... for years?` said David, a little surprised at hearing the name.`

Malci Shaw had had an unfortunate relationship with a woman who when drunk became acutely paranoid and depressive. This was understandable, but was then compounded with serious suicidal tendencies and on such occasions and in order to relinquish and abrogate any responsibility for her just in case she should attempt any form of self destruction, he would simply drink more than her and thereby in his eyes release himself from any direct responsibility for her actions.

However, on this particular occasion, the woman in question had become extremely drunk and after arguing with Malci decided, she wanted to drive back to her parent's house, which was some distance away and possibly kill herself on the journey. Malci, unfortunately, had not drunk very much on the night in question and for her own safety and that of other road users, he had taken away her keys and kept her locked in his flat with the intention of keeping her there until she had sobered up. There then commenced another argument, which became extremely vociferous and exceptionally noisy and at one stage Malci threw Carol's (the lady in question) mobile phone out of his flat window to stop her calling the police. Unfortunately for Malci a nearby resident who had witnessed the whole event and fearing a possible serious escalation of hostilities, if that were possible and assuming the worst conceivable outcome, called the police anyway and they arrived to find Carol ranting on that she had been kidnapped by Malci and that he had raped against her will (which I don't think is what she meant to say as I had always assumed that was taken for granted anyway). However, despite her profoundly intoxicated condition she still had the presence of mind to cite the afore mentioned mobile phone which lay shattered outside the flat window as evidence of his actions and intentions and he was subsequently arrested on a charge of holding her against her will. (The rape charge was later dropped through lack of physical evidence and factual clarity).

Unfortunately, the forces of fair play were not with Malci this night. He had been arrested many times before for various minor offences, all of which he had pleaded not guilty to, but was nevertheless found guilty of. However, on this occasion Carol's father an ex-CID officer of thirty years' service (a fact unbeknown to Malci at the time and a man who never took prisoners and had a severe dislike for Malci anyway) decided to exercise a little bit of the old pals act. He suggested to the Crown Prosecution Service (they owed him a favour anyway) that maybe he should also be charged (under a lesser-known section of the police and criminal evidence act 1984) as someone who also posed a permanent threat to society in general and women in particular. If found guilty of the main charge the additional element of the charge would be considered at sentencing. Sure enough, he was found guilty of abduction and false imprisonment and the wilful destruction of her mobile phone. After the judge had given the matter his deepest consideration, he was sentenced to be held at her majesty's pleasure until such times as he was considered to be of no further threat to society. The decision on any future release date would be decided by a review board, which would reconsider his case once a year. This effectively was a life sentence for smashing a phone and trying to save his girlfriend's life and he served six years for it. A result for Carol's dad a vindictive bastard at the best of times according to his wife and a lesson to us all.

`...So did I,` replied Ashley somewhat effusively, `but it would appear they released him early for being a good chap, so he's back here - celebrating.`

`Is Sarah here?` enquired David sharply. His normally temperate if occasionally fractious demeanour had deteriorated abruptly at the mention of Malci Shaw's name. Ashley pointed sheepishly in the direction of the crowd, which were now even louder than when he had first entered the bar and were now becoming visibly agitated.

`What the hell is she doing back with him?` exclaimed David showing signs of being a little distressed at the possibility of his sister and Malci Shaw resuming their relationship.

`No idea,` replied Ashley. `I haven't spoken to her tonight,` this was all kicking off when I popped in for a quiet pint. He smiled at his sardonic witticism and lifted his wavering empty glass to David again, in an unspoken gesture to buy him a drink.

`OK get me a lager then,` said David. `Thanks.`

`Righty Oh,` mumbled Ashley turning back to the bar and attempting to attract the attention of Rosie the barmaid who was serving another customer. Rosie, was not particularly pretty, not in any sense of the word. In fact, she was very possibly ugly, but nevertheless still strangely attractive in the way that only street whore's can be, having an indefinable case hardened sexuality. This was what

Ashley had found so hard to resist since the very first time he saw her. The first impression always did the most damage and the first response always left the lasting memory. She had succeeded on both counts.

He had given this paradoxical proclivity serious thought on many occasions during the time he had been frequenting the pub. The conclusion that he had eventually come to - after in-depth self-analysis - was that his private and public school education had subliminally suppressed his natural tendency for a challenge and that the surfeit of attractive females, something that he had always found intimidating, had done nothing but strengthen this repression. This in turn had triggered his inability to interact socially, particularly with attractive well-mannered women. Exposure to the more earthy qualities of lowly accessible barmaids very quickly alleviated this problem. Rosie's short black leather mini skirt and white chiffon see through blouse covered the absolute bare minimum necessary in order to maintain some sort of level of decency and propriety, but still exposed sufficient veiled flesh to attract men from far and wide with a mission. The allure of perception of the unavailable compressively overwhelmed the reality of accessibility and easy virtue.

Rosie's indolently vicarious demeanour would have been better suited to an eighteenth century gin house of ill repute rather than a twentieth century pub, but then in many respects there really wasn't any difference. Remove the gaming machines, ponderous music and chemically enhanced lager and you could easily be transported back to a Hogarthian plateau where morals and common decency hovered at a level not dissimilar to today. This created a profoundly morbid and pervasive tableau of the rise and decline of English sociality.

She looked at him and smiled encouragingly as she did with every customer and mouthed a few inaudible words to reassure him that she had not forgotten him. He felt flattered by this visual acknowledgement of his existence and sufficiently satisfied to patiently await his turn. The physiology of the subtle manipulation of his sensibilities by the use of a   beguiling almost entrancing smile was not entirely lost on him and he smiled to himself with   the reassuring self-satisfaction of knowing they were playing their own private game within a much larger game.

`I thought that was all over?` said David who was still coming to terms with the unexpected reappearance of Malci Shaw; his mind had shunted back a few years and he was slowly recalling vague elements of events from that period.

`Evidently not dear boy,` replied Ashley, who although now beginning to slur his words a little,   still retained a certain varsity cadence faintly reminiscent of his refined education.

`What are they doing?` asked David whose curiosity was now growing more intense by the second.

`Don't know,` replied Ashley, who felt guilty about lying to his friend as he did in fact have a good idea what was going on as he had been watching and listening to the progressive intensification of interest in the centre of the room since he arrived and had also caught some garbled snatches of innuendo from onlookers returning to the bar. Nevertheless, he was not going to be the one to convey this blather to David.   He wondered where the line between honesty and naivety would be drawn and was this something that he should worry about.   He could hardly be accused of Jesuitical casuistry for saying nothing,   as far as he was concerned he was not trying to deceive, merely to avoid.

`Probably just getting a tadge inebriated and having a laugh,` continued Ashley. `That's what we do on Friday nights round here, but I'm staying out of his way. He doesn't like me very much. I have no idea why, he just does.` Ashley believed that his policy of adopting a non-confrontational lowly profile should sufficiently distance him from any direct altercation with Shaw and to a large degree it worked.

Rosie, who had now finished serving another customer, sauntered towards the end of the bar where Ashley was standing, smiling and beguiling him as she approached like a lion mesmerising her prey.

`And what would the master like?` she drawled in her most provocative tone. Ashley smiled back and fawned coquettish almost adolescent surprise at her ambiguously phrased question.

`Ah! A serving wench at last methinks! My pot to filleth up.` He exclaimed this in an exaggerated Shakespearian iambic pentameter for extra effect, then leaned a little closer over the bar and continued the conversation, in a softer tenor. Any social repression he may have been suffering firmly put asunder, now consigned to the dustbin of experience. `Rosie,' he paused, 'have I told you lately what beautiful eyes you have?` all the while firmly maintaining visual contact with her slightly larger than average cleavage.

Why the fuck don't they talk to me instead of my tits, Rosie wondered. This propensity annoyed her intensely, she was a person as well as a barmaid and surely, she should be accorded some sort of social nicety. She knew why she dressed the way she did, but that was just the theatricality. Didn't they understand this?

She placed her forefinger strategically under his chin and slowly lifted his head so that he was looking directly at her face and with a well-practiced flintiness cultivated through many joyous years of self-inflicted servitude and reactionary verbal abrasion she whispered with endearing but darkly shaded naivety `No not today you haven't, but you will have to do a little better than that if you want to have your wicked way with a poor little serving wench like little me.` She waggled her breasts at him.

`Playing hard to get are we?` replied Ashley with a delicate touch of acceptable sarcasm, but totally devoid of the harsh derision that normally accompanied a disdainful comment. He had noticed on many occasions how quickly some men revert to juvenile abuse when a crude attempt at a sexually oblique advance, laden with testosterone and control issues was rejected. Rosie just smiled and said nothing.

There was no underlying subtext or hidden agenda and she didn't feel threatened, which was not always the case.

Ashley's normally fragile confidence in the presence of women grew in leaps and bounds in the presence of Rosie. She threw him a little titbit and he gobbled it up. Ashley suddenly became distracted by a small bead of sweat that was slowly trickling down from her temple to her cheek. Rosie's eye twisted from left to right curious to see what precisely he was gazing at. She knew he was not looking directly at her eyes.. and for some reason this caused her a little concern.

`Could I have two pints of your finest grog?` Ashley interjected, `for my friend and I fair damsel and move your little arse while you're about it.` Ashley's confidence level had grown a point or two.

`Yes master,` she humbly replied, continuing to play her role. His eyes were now focused back on hers, as best as he could manage considering his state of inebriation. The trickle of sweat on Rosie's face had finished its journey having run out of sufficient quantum to continue further.

`And which finest grog would that be sir?` asked Rosie humbly.

`What have you got?` replied Ashley smiling. 'And none of the chemical shit,'

Rosie smiled back, looked down at her large cleavage and then looked up again.

`Black Death! Everything else is off.`

`Oh that's a shame,` said Ashley shaming a little disheartened shrug laced with innuendo.

`Would you like that?` asked Rosie coyly.

`That would be splendid,` replied Ashley.

`So two large pints is that all?` she asked.

`Yes that will be all for now thank you,` replied Ashley politely. Rosie smiled and walked away very slowly, deliberately wiggling her arse as she went. When she got to the pump, she turned to pour the two drinks and pouted at Ashley.

`You could have done something about that?` said David.

`I'm working on it,` replied Ashley, his brain still engaged elsewhere. David noticed who Ashley was looking at and who he was obviously referring to and tapped him on the shoulder to attract his attention. Ashley turned to him.

`Not her, Sarah,` said David, but Ashley just held his hands up as if to say, "How!"

`She's driving the car mate,` replied Ashley in his defence. `It's up to her where she steers its.` David had no option but to acknowledge that Ashley was not Sarah's keeper and definitely not responsible for her.. he did however wonder about the obtuse metaphor.

`Where's Harry?` asked David now sounding more concerned than just curious.

`Big brother? exclaimed Ashley thinking about the question for a few moments. `He was here earlier. The three of them had a bit of a barny then Harry left, I think.`

Ashley returned to watching Rosie, and David looked at Ashley a little disparagingly before walking towards the crowd and starting to push his way through. He turned briefly to look back at Ashley once more and Ashley shouted back to him.

`Sorry mate, nothing I could do.` He enunciated the words very slowly, but David couldn't hear them clearly over the noise of the crowd.

`Brilliant,` mouthed David, `...brilliant.` He mumbled it again under his breath. Rosie returned and Ashley paid her and took a sip from his pint. David continued to make his way to the centre of the huddle and after much jesting and jeering from the crowd came to a small clearing. Malci was standing with a cigarette in one hand and a pint of beer in the other. He was obviously very drunk and appeared almost demented, very intimidating, indolently arrogant and dangerous. He was swaying a little but managed to stay on

the spot.   Sarah Marshall was kneeling before him
performing oral sex.   Malci tapped the cigarette ash onto
Sarah's head, laughed into the air to further humiliate her and
then took another slurp of his beer. He enjoyed entertaining
the crowd on this his homecoming day.   Sarah caught a
glimpse of her brother out of the corner of her eye and turned
slightly towards him.

`Stop!` Shouted David with a sonorous resonation that
carried over the top of the baying cacophonous mass,
piercing the barbarous rabble and as the word reverberated
around the room the whole crowd slowly froze and suddenly
became eerily quiet. Sarah stopped what she was doing and
turned to look directly at David and for a few seconds her
expression changed to one of complete and utter hopelessness
and despair.

`Why are you doing this?` shouted David, although the
room was still hushed and his bellowing voice seemed to
echo round the room.   His repulsion   by the sickening
vertiginous level of humiliation and depravity that she had so
willingly subjected herself too was as clearly palpable as the
sudden realisation by the crowd that it too was witnessing
and a party to an appalling display of sexual degeneracy more
indicative of the behaviour of a pack of wild animals than
people.

The crowd waited and watched in silence for Sarah to
answer, but she was looking at the floor and thinking about
what David had just said - for this was more degrading than
even she could have imagined. How had she arrived at this
point in her life? This question went around and around her
head bouncing off the inside of her skull, first to her ears then
her brain then her eyes then back to her ears, she couldn't
make any sense of it until in a brief moment of lucidity she
forced herself to look up at David and totally drained of any
emotion she quietly answered...

`It makes him happy, that's all I want to do. Make him
happy. Is that so wrong?`   David was suddenly aware of a
strange resonance in the tone of her voice and the choice of

words which reminded him of something from long ago in their childhood, but he just couldn't remember what.

In the midst of all the commotion, she forced a smile of resigned self-loathing humiliation. Her eyes begged forgiveness and understanding, but David just turned away as the crowd burst back into life and began jeering and screaming again, even louder than before, slowly rising to a tumultuous crescendo of choral depravity, a shout of defiance to the heavens and damnation to society. Malci smiled with arrogant satisfaction and elation and then he shouted..

'The warrior has returned!' The crowd roared out in approbation. There were those in the room who thought it was better to be a chicken running with the fox than a dead chicken. Malci held up his beer glass and waved it around to another loud cheer from the crowd, revelling in the artificial adulation and respect he now commanded, only to clumsily spill a few splashes of beer onto Sarah. Malci looked down at her, sneered and grabbed hold of his erect penis and plunged it towards her face. She guided it home and looked up at Malci, he grinned with a menace she knew only too well and continued with the theatrical depravity.

She was no longer a part of this, she was now elevated above the bedlam of medieval debauched mental carnage that surrounded her. The contemptuous taunting grew louder, the crowd cried out for more. David turned back for one final glance at Sarah. This was her choice. Nobody had forced her to endure the ultimate humiliation of prostrating her body and soul on a shitty, stinking beer soaked floor in the middle of a back street smoke filled piss hole in front of an audience of morally bankrupt drunken degenerates. This was her choice.

David could feel the sodden carpet beneath his feet, pulling him down to the floor like a sticky magnet, resisting his enraged attempt to escape. Each step was an effort to detach his shoes from the floor as he made his way back to the bar.. She does have a choice, he said to himself, we all have a choice in life. Most of us do what we have to do, in order to do what we want to do and maybe we don't want to do it, but it becomes necessary to survive. Nobody made her do this, nobody forced her, and this was her chosen option, her choice. She could have walked away, if she wanted to, but she didn't. Therefore, she must be in control he reasoned. It was easy for him to think this way, he wasn't responsible for anybody, he didn't depend on anybody and nobody depended on him he was a free agent who went where he pleased, did what he wanted, but he didn't really understand. He moved back through the crowd to where Ashley was standing. Ashley sipped his beer and carefully held up the pint he had bought David.

`I really am sorry mate but it was out of my control. I got here and...`Ashley stopped talking realising that there was nothing of value he could say. David took the glass from Ashley and gazed at him, saddened with a sense of turbid moral rectitude. He slowly lifted the glass to his lips and swallowed a large mouthful of beer. His eyes now fixed on some indeterminate point in space. His thoughts flashed back to the events of twenty years ago and how they had inextricably set in motion the inexplicable trail of events that had brought them all to this moment. He wondered how much more emotional devastation they might cause before eventually culminating in something he dared not contemplate. His incontrovertible belief in the random nature of human existence had always reasoned that the convergence of circumstances that had brought Sarah here on this night were entirely due to the uncontrollable hand of fate and had nothing what so ever to do with a god, but even that closely held conviction was beginning to falter and fall by the wayside. Whose hand would inflict such demonstrable anguish and humiliation on two innocent children? Surely not a god the creator of life, a deity who trafficked in morality, but if not God or chance, who was it who controlled this destiny...

He turned back towards Ashley his eyes filled with the palpable despondently he felt in his heart and quietly muttered `I know.` he looked straight into Ashley's eyes,

`I've always known.` then he threw the rest of the pint down his throat and walked out of the door, away from the incarnate madness that was bleaching his soul.

Chapter 5

1970. The first experience.

Harry was awoken in the early hours of the morning by his body's insatiable demand for water. He was aware he had a desire, but at his age did not fully appreciate the implications. The already slowing failing ability of his pancreas to produce sufficient insulin was a problem caused by his mother feeding him fresh cow's milk when they had lived on a farm in a hippy commune just after he was born. It was discovered many years later that the consumption of untreated cow's milk by an infant, exposed them to what was then an as yet unidentified component in the milk that would eventually trigger an autoimmune reaction in the body. This like so many things in his life was preordained and beyond his control.

He slipped out of his warm bed into the cold night air and tip toed as quietly as he could from his bedroom, across the hall landing, slowly making his way towards the door of his parents' bedroom. The bare floorboards groaned eerily almost as if they were in redemptive pain. If was the same kind of whispery noise his grandfather made not long before died.

Harry stopped for a moment unsure whether he should continue. He was used to the creaking sounds and the stillness of the air, but there was something different about tonight. This was a journey he had made many times, but as far as he could remember, he had never before experienced such foreboding thoughts of apprehension and trepidation as he felt tonight. Deep in the firmament of his soul, he sensed that many things would soon change, possibly forever, but not even in his wildest thoughts could he ever have imagined how they would change or what the final outcome would be.

Despite carefully transferring his weight from one foot to the other as he warily navigated his way towards the bathroom, the wooden floorboards - which had shrunk and twisted over the years - still continued to murmur a slow and painful deathly creak as if they were to about to open up and swallow him into a cavernous hollow below, but they did not. He stood perfectly still, frozen to the spot and for a few seconds almost stopped breathing, but to no avail. He could now feel his heart pounding so loudly that surely someone would hear it, but no one did so he continued his journey. He walked slower than before , as he had no wish to disturb his parents. He had however momentarily forgotten that ultimately he would have to cross their bedroom to reach his destination and unless they were sound asleep, which they were not, there was little chance of achieving that without them noticing him. As he drew closer to the door, he heard muffled conversation coming from the bedroom and stood briefly mesmerised by the warm light that he could see flickering out from around the edges of bedroom door, which was ajar. The unsteady splutter of the candle light burnt fitfully, occasionally flashing out across the landing floor, casting curiously elongated dragon like shapes around the hallway and then without warning the shadows would haphazardly fly up the walls and sweep out across the hallway like a giant's arms soaring down to gather him up and carry him off to a fiery magical kingdom of monsters and demons.

He remembered the stories his mother used to read to him each night before he went to sleep. He was much younger then and innocently impressionable, but despite his mother's valiant attempts at bizarre gravelly throated inflections and vague, incongruous, tonal nuance's he was never genuinely frightened by her dark tales about the people who lived in the black forests of countries that he had never heard of and he wasn't frightened now. Sometimes he would feign fear and anxious concern for the heroes and protagonists' but this was only to encourage the storyteller and engender further tales. He had already learnt the power of subtle sycophancy and obsequious comments, but this made him feel guilty for he knew he was abusing an unspoken trust.

He knew they were just silly make believe stories, but the memories they left behind were indelibly imprinted in his brain for the rest of his life. Tiny creases on tissue paper that can never be truly erased and they were never far from his thoughts whether sleeping or awake. All the fears and concerns he had held for soldiers of fortune who having safety returned from the war, with knapsacks of gold and tinder boxes, but unexpectedly, had fallen foul of the witches spell, while almost within sight of home. All the hopes of a safe deliverance for the hero from the evil that always skulked in every darkened corner and was always there.

He rubbed his eyes for he was still barely awake but he was thirsty, very thirsty and this drove him forward. The maddened shadow marionettes continued their dance of death, but he took little notice, for he felt less fear of the unknown, than the known.

Gently, he pushed open the bedroom door, knowing that the bathroom, his final destination was on the other side of his parent's bedroom and he reminded himself that he must pass through their room and must not disturb them if at all possible. Normally they would be asleep but tonight it was different. As he entered the bedroom, he could see more candles burning in various places around the room each illuminating a small area before the light gently faded to darkness only for another area to be re illuminated by the next candle. There was an ethereal quality to the room he could only ever remember encountering in his dreams, however this illusion was quickly dispersed when he saw a man, a man he didn't know standing on the far side of the bed. The stranger was naked and was his holding his mother's head in his hands and moving rhythmically backwards and forwards. His mother was kneeling down on the bed with both hands holdings the man's waist. Harry was curious and as he entered the room. A little further in, he could now see his stepfather behind his mother holding her

64

hips and he too was also moving rhythmically. He noticed his mother's breasts swaying erratically. This unusual arrangement was not something he had encountered before and he was bewildered and confused on diverse levels of comprehension by what he was witnessing. His primary intention was to slake his thirst and he continued his passage across the bedroom trying to ignore what was happening, but he was suddenly brought to a sharp halt when his father realised he was in the room.

`What do you want!` His father harshly barked.

`Can I get some water please dad, I'm very thirsty,` replied Harry apprehensively.

`Can't you ever stay in your room for more than five minutes without causing a bloody nuisance. You could have got the water before you went to bed` His father was obviously not pleased by the untimely intervention. Harry stood perfectly still not wishing to cause further offence.

`I'm sorry I wasn't thirsty then,` replied Harry sheepishly in his defence, for he was too young to comprehend the exigencies of forbearance and patience. He only understood his overwhelming desire to slake his thirst. Nothing else was of any importance.

`You should have got it earlier,` his stepfather harshly replied. Harry couldn't understand this as all he knew was that he felt the need now.

The inquisitorial nature of the reply began to concern Harry, he began to wish he had not entered the room. `I wasn't thirsty...` he repeated nervously, but he didn't finish.

`I'll give you a bloody good hiding in the morning, that'll stop you wandering about all night.`

`I'm sorry. I only wanted a drink,` replied Harry apologetically now becoming a little fearful of the repercussions, the like of which he had experienced before.

`Get the water and be quick about it,` snapped his stepfather.

`I'm sorry,` replied Harry. He thought about asking who the stranger was, but changed his mind.

The stranger took no notice of Harry and continued with what he was doing with Harry's mother. For some reason she seemed to be completely unaware that Harry was even in the room and appeared to be preoccupied and completely oblivious to what was happening.

As he hastily made his way to the bathroom, he noticed a strange heavy sweet aroma in the room. He recalled smelling something similar on a number of occasions in the past, but he couldn't remember exactly when. He turned the tap on, filled his tumbler and took a quick sip before exiting across the bedroom once more as fast as he could, but mindful not to spill the water. He took one last glance at the stranger as he left.

`Don't come back tonight and shut the door,` his stepfather barked as he left the room. There was a tone to his voice which he had only heard two or three times before usually when his stepfather was drunk and on those occasions he had often resorted to violence and had beaten him.

`No father,` he replied apologetically as he closed the door and made his way back to his bedroom now concerned about the future consequences of his visit to the bathroom. When he had returned to his bedroom he didn't get into bed and thought he would go and talk to Sarah, but instead decided to hide in the large painted wooden box in the corner of the room where he fell asleep amongst his toys. He felt safe inside the box not exposed to things that were beyond his control. In his dreams, he remembered his baby sister Caroline who was born just over a year ago but had left after only six months. He didn't understand why she had gone, all he knew was that his new father didn't love him or his sister Sarah the same as he had loved Caroline.

Chapter 6

It was an early December morning, the day after Carla's funeral and snow was falling heavily in the back garden of Nigel's house. Tony had opened one of the French doors just wide enough to allow him to feel the cold air now swirling with snowflakes, some of which blew on to his face. He desperately needed to feel something, some form of tangible sadness that he could relate to, something that would bring the physical reality to a day when he had so far only experienced a complete lack of sensation. Each flake landing on his face immediately dissolved into a small droplet of water and ran down his cheek. As he wiped them away he wondered why these droplets were not real tears, maybe artificial ones were all he was entitled. Was this the payback for walking away he wondered, he would never know for certain.

Her death and subsequent funeral had not had the effect on him he thought it would have and although fourteen years had passed since their divorce, he felt a sense of guilt for this emotional omission. He knew he should have felt differently less insensate, but he was not sure how. What troubled him most was a complete absence of compassion for the woman who was after all the mother of his children; this did not sit easily with him. He could understand falling out of love with her, that was a part of life, but this was something different

They had both made serious errors of judgement and trust, which had caused the irrevocable breakdown of their marriage, but these, had only become known long after it had become too late to make amends. Tony was looking for some kind of redemption and reassurance that he hadn't become immune to his own sensibilities, but where could he find that now?

The room was lit by two lamp standards, one by a large old oak desk and the other by the armchair where Tony was sitting, where he had been sitting all night. The room's dark oak panelling and the soft orangey glow of the lamps only enhanced the pervading sense of fading clarity that Tony was feeling. Tony and Carla had been married for twenty-six years before the divorce, but he had never entirely understood what had happened prior to their marriage as well as a large part of the period when they were married. The words never spoken that should have been, words that could have answered so many questions, were the consequence of his cowardice and restraint, the actions that should have been taken but were not, actions that could have changed so many things were his errors of judgement.

The faint palliative sound of the early morning birdsong, heavily muffled by the snow was broken only by the gentle ticking of a grandfather clock. The chorus of life, inexorably, relentlessly and with a calm indifference, slowly counting down the remaining seconds, minutes, hours and days of the unexpired term of each of their lives. The clock sounded patient and yet arrogant and it had every right to be, for it would be around long after they were all gone.

How many more years would he see he wondered and would he ever know the truth. Tony stared out into the garden, he felt tired, but sleep didn't make him any less tired anymore. Nigel - Tony and Carla's son, a man with a normally jovial disposition, but not so today, opened the drawing room door and quietly entered the room, not being sure whether his father was awake or asleep.

`Are you OK dad?` He whispered, loud enough to be heard if Tony was awake, but not too loud in case he was asleep.

`I'm fine,` Tony replied, `you get back to bed.`

`Couldn't sleep either,` said Nigel by way of explanation, `thought I'd make a cup some tea. Would you like one?`

`No I'm OK,` replied Tony, `thanks anyway.` He waved his half full whiskey tumbler and smiled at Nigel. `This will keep me going, could do with some ice though.` Tony had been steadily drinking since they got back from the funeral at four o'clock the previous day, but the whiskey appeared to have had little effect on him. It may have dulled his senses, but it hadn't desensitised him to the previous day's events and it had done very little to erase the thoughts, doubts and feelings of self-recriminations that were running around his head and which were the primary reason for drinking the whiskey in the first place. Furthermore, it had produced the opposite effect to that which he had intended as it had kept him awake to contemplate further on what had happened leading up to yesterday's events. So it had failed in concept and delivery. There was little reprieve from the constant rerun of the memories and revelations of the last forty years that kept flashing across his mind like the marketing trailer for some forthcoming cinematic attraction.

`Right,` said Nigel, `no sooner said than....` as he moved towards the kitchen which was just off of the drawing room. `Sandwich?` he enquired as he entered the kitchen.

`No, no I'm OK, really. Thanks. How is Katie by the way? Wasn't sure how she'd cope with the funeral and everything.. `

`Fine, she'd sleep through anything,` replied Nigel from the kitchen.... `Only wish I could these days, quite envious really. Spend most of my night's half-awake trying to plan what I have to do the next day to avert another disaster and when I do actually wake up I'm still tired and worried that I may have forgotten something so I'm worse off than I was before I went to bed. I suppose that's the price you pay to have a decent life and stay in the race.`

`It's the beginning of getting old you know.. ` replied Tony.

`What forgetting things?` asked Nigel

`Not sleeping. The Alzheimer's kicks in a little later.` Tony smiled to himself.

`Now you've given me something else to worry about,` replied Nigel mockingly.

`No need to, when it kicks in you won't remember a thing, that's the upside.` Tony smiled to himself again. The diversion was a small mental digression in which he was happy to indulge   as a   welcome respite from the final lingering remnants of a story now nearly over, although the closing lines had yet to be written.

`What's the downside?` asked Nigel a little cautiously.

`Don't know, I can't remember!` replied Tony joyfully. It was an old punch line, but he liked it and he liked it even better when he got it right.   Spontaneous jokes and asides were never really his forte.

Nigel smiled to himself. There was a sense of closure beginning to emerge which brought him some release from the thoughts that filled his mind and the concerns he had for his father.

`She never seems to have a care in world,` said Nigel changing the subject, `nothing seems to faze her,  the only thing she worries about is that horse, which costs me a bloody fortune.  But I suppose it's worth it just to see her really happy after all that's happened.`

`Children are much stronger than you think.` replied Tony standing up and walking over to the French doors. He closed the one that was ajar and stood and stared into the garden looking at the snow that had settled.

`Resilient, they're just more resilient than we are,` replied Nigel walking back into the drawing room with a cup of tea, a sandwich and glass of ice. He passed the ice to Tony who put three cubes into his whiskey, and then sat down in an armchair. Tony sat back down and took out his cigarettes.

`Is it OK if I...?` asked Tony waving a packet of cigarettes.

`Off course, we both smoke in here, don't worry about it,` replied Nigel. Tony lit up a cigarette picked up an ashtray from the table and put it on the arm of his chair.

`Yes you're probably right` said Tony They seem to be able to absorb huge amounts of heartache and pain and still manage to bounce back, bit like a boxers old punch bag, punched a thousand times from every angle, but still looks just the same from the outside, a little frayed maybe. . . . It's almost as if losing someone has no real effect on them at all. As if.. they can't comprehend the permanency of loss.

`Oh I think it does,` replied Nigel, `the damage is inside where it can't be seen.  But the hurt's still there  hidden away for a while, but always there it never goes away.`

Tony took another sip from his whiskey glass. `Do you think we all have  hurt hidden away?` He got up and wandered over to the French window again.

`You tell me,` said Nigel, `How do you feel about what happened you've never spoken vary much about it?`

Tony turned to Nigel and whether the whiskey had weakened his normally reserved demeanour or if it had heightened his perception of his own inadequacy, he wasn't sure, but he replied with an uncharacteristic intensity that Nigel had not seen before, not for many years at least.

`Rage!...` replied Tony. His fingers tightened around the glass and the muscles in his arm tensed. `Rage and anguish for being blind and naïve; and bitter disappointment for failing them and you. That's how I feel. It's like, something that happened to somebody else, to other people I didn't know and I was just a spectator watching this story unfold. Then suddenly somebody speaks to me and I realise I'm actually in this, I am actually a part of this catastrophic nightmare and I'm in the middle of everything, but somehow I managed to miss the beginning. I don't remember how I missed it, but I did and now I feel responsible because I wasn't paying attention and I should have been and I'm still totally confused by what has happened because I just don't understand.`

`It wasn't your fault,` replied Nigel, with an inflection clearly demonstrating he knew who he thought was to blame, but he stopped himself from elaborating any further on this particular day and left the clearly unambiguous indictment hanging in the air.

Tony looked at Nigel with an expression of sadness, wretchedness and remorse. What happened had undoubtedly damaged everybody including Nigel to one degree or another and no amount of soul searching, recrimination or reproach would change that. It would have been easy for him to just succumb to the generally accepted version of events, but he always fought against the light when there was still a tiny element of doubt in his mind and he needed to purge this doubt from his memory before he could be completely sure of what had happened. Then the whole matter could be laid to rest. If he could not do that, it would never go away.

`Oh I know that now,` replied Tony, `but it doesn't stop me from thinking that I should have known, that it was my responsibility to know?` Tony emanated a palpable sense of guilt that had obviously been playing on his mind for a long time.

`But you didn't and nothing can change that now,` replied Nigel.

`Probably not,` said Tony, `but the trouble is that's the way my life has always been.` Just when he thought he had everything planned and he understood how the game was played somebody always came along and snatched the ball away and ran off with it. He would be left standing there in the middle of nowhere knowing all the rules, all the little dodges and tricks, all the little things that can't be taught, but he couldn't play anymore because someone had stolen the ball. Then one day he realised he had been playing a different game altogether to everybody else anyway and he never quite understood why. He began to wonder if it was him that was out of sync with everybody else and maybe that was why he was always the odd one out. That's when self-doubt started to creep into the equation. That is when he realised how pathetic and lamentable the whole situation really was. He began to wonder if some hidden force had conspired against him, but that was just paranoia. No, this was just down to him not paying attention plain and simple, no excuses.

`Maybe her death has affected you more than you thought it would,` added Nigel, `maybe it will affect all of us  more than we think one day. We're all putting on this  brave front but...` Nigel didn't go any further.

Maybe you're right thought Tony, death does tend to make you focus on the really important things in life. That's when you really start to think about God and mortality when other people die. Especially the ones close to you, the ones you really care about. You wonder whether you did enough for them when they were still around, whether you could have done something that would have made their lives a little better, easier, maybe they asked you to do something once, a long time ago and you promised to do it, but you never did and now you never will.

`Do you have any  regrets dad?` asked Nigel.

`Some yes, of course I do.` replied Tony, he thought back to the things he had probably said when they were having an argument, spiteful malicious little jibes, pathetic little stabs of venomous bile designed solely to inflict pain, but without any real justification and yet the moment the words left his mouth he knew he had overstepped the mark, but out of sheer stubbornness he refused to retract or apologise and the scar is left just sitting there like a festering cancer quietly gathering momentum year after year till one day... Tony took another sip of whiskey. This was self-purging catharsis, which maybe everybody goes through at a time like this. The guilt of you still being alive and them being dead. Always the same question why them not me? But he did not feel that this time. In the end, time is the only separation between life and death and that passes so fast that it hardly seems worthwhile worrying about it. We would all be there soon enough anyway.

Every funeral a sharp reminder that you are one-step closer to the dark reapers next sweep through the golden meadow we call life. You can skip over the blade as he thrashes it through the tall grass and cuts it down to size. You can laugh behind his back because he missed you that time, but every jump saps your strength just a little and every time you land, it's a little heavier than before and you feel a little weaker than you were. He knows you are mocking him, but he does not care. You can laugh as much as you like because he missed you this time and sometimes he will even laugh with you. He may even applaud you for your temerity and your bravery, because he can see the funny side to it all. He understands absolutely the pointless paradox of life and we still don't. We think there is a reason, but there isn't, there is only accountability for now. All the rest is nothing. He will get you though, if not today, maybe tomorrow or the next day, but he will get you. Just as sure as God made little apples, he will get you in the end.

Eventually you become a little more tolerant of other people's shortcomings, not as impatient as you once used to be when something didn't go quite the way you expected and you come to terms with the inevitability and reality of life and begin to absorb conflict instead of deflecting it. Every crisis renders you a little wearier and a little bit weaker than before and then one day you find you don't have the strength or the energy to resist anymore, just the ability to understand. It is God's way of preparing us for what is in store.

`I regret not being able to believe in a God more than I do,` said Tony.

`I didn't know you were religious?` asked Nigel sounding surprised.

`No I'm not, but don't get those two imposters confused,` replied Tony with unexpected consternation.

`I don't understand` said Nigel curiously.

`Evelyn Waugh said religion was all trickery, witchcraft, hypocrisy and superstition and I'm inclined to agree with him on that, but God, that's something quite different. In that, I probably do believe, but only in the context of a finely balanced equation. I still feel that this subscription is an hypocrisy to everything I have seen in my life.` Tony spoke with surprising adroitness and clarity considering his inebriated state.

`So do you blame God for all that has happened?` enquired Nigel cautiously.

`No that would be too easy,` replied Tony, `and anyway to blame God I would need to have believed in him for most of my life without reservation, which I haven't. If I had then the question would then have to be "do I still believe?" and that would have been just a little too convenient and tritely disingenuous, so on balance I choose not to blame God whether he does exist or not.`

Nigel thought about that for a few moments. `Are you sure you don't want anything?` he asked, tactfully attempting to change the course of conversation. He realised he had lost interest in a discussion on the merits of ecclesiastical morality a subject he had always thought to be dubious at best anyway and definitely not one to be entered into lightly with friends or relations especially at this time or in these circumstances. Religion was a subject he never liked to dwell on too long with anybody he cared for. It tended to bring out the darker side of everybody and was never much fun. The old adage about avoiding religion and politics at a dinner party never truer.

`No thanks this will do fine.` Tony gestured to the cigarette and whiskey.

`I thought Katie handled it well,` said Nigel.

`Boarding school makes you strong,` replied Tony, `and self-reliant. You begin to understand the concept of loss very quickly when you live away from home.`

There was a tiny hint of regret in his voice for although he had been fortunate enough and considered himself to be very lucky to have attended boarding schooling, he had missed the cohesive nature of a physical proximity to his parents during his younger years and he realised that more now than when he was younger.

`I suppose it teaches you the real value of independence? It did for me anyway,` replied Nigel.

`If I'd had the money... I think I would have sent you all to boarding school,` replied Tony. `Maybe then things would have turned out differently?` He had been earning enough to send Nigel and David to private school, but had not been in that position ten years earlier when Harry and Sarah had started school.

`I think the problem started long before that,` replied Nigel.

`Yes you're probably right,` replied Tony quietly.

`Katie loved her very much,` said Nigel.

`Yes I know she did,` said Tony. `I remember a few years ago when she was very young about four or maybe five she told me she loved me "loads and loads," and that I was her "favourite grandpa," but she loved Grandma just a little bit more than me because Grandma understood how she felt... and she had lots of shoes.`

`Yes, I remember her saying that,` replied Nigel, `never quite understood what she meant though, the shoes bit yes, but the other... but then she's has always had   this disarmingly quality of saying exactly what she is thinking and speaking her mind as she sees it. Sometimes a little abrupt maybe and not always particularly palatable, but then I suppose all children intuitively tell the perfect truth before they begin to realise they have to accommodate just a tiny element of polite diplomacy and economy in order to avoid offending people.`

`It's a bit ironic when you think about it,` queried Tony philosophically. `First we instil the importance of total honesty and then we sabotage the integrity of the lesson by asking them to be a little less exact and maybe leave a thing or two out and colour what they say with a little obsequiousness.   Then we wonder why they become confused... but then you must have been through all of this already?`

`A little, but with her being away most of the time she seems to have learnt that at school anyway,` replied Nigel.

`I think mothers always communicate better with their granddaughters,` mused Tony. No barriers or parental pressure, must be something to do with protecting the maternal bloodline I guess? They see the person inside the child that is who they talk to. It was me that Carla never opened up to, that's what I never understood. I did try but... she was always distant and the closer you tried to get, the further she pulled away. There was always something she would never talk about. I always thought it was Caroline, but I was wrong. Over the years, I saw that whatever it was, it was eating away at her, but there was nothing I could do. I don't suppose there was anything anyone could do. Towards the end I think she came to terms with it and began looking for.., I don't know... some sort of contrition, atonement maybe, no that's the wrong word, absolution that's what she needed, what she wanted, but from what? I never realised, not till much later.

`Katie's innocence may have actually helped,` said Nigel, `I think she reminded mum just how vulnerable children really are and how much they need love. That was a second chance for her, an opportunity to put things right possibly.`

`I did notice she had more patience and time for Katie, she learnt to listen and trade secrets for riddles. Katie could sense that, maybe that is why they got on so well and Carla could see Katie was still untainted, uncorrupted by the betrayals of life.` replied Tony.

`She has a free spirit which I find incredibly infectious...` replied Nigel with just a small hint of admiration, `...it makes me feel good just to be with her, to see her laughing at everything, just watching her sometimes. I only wish I could be like that. Children can inspire you when you become a little weary with life...`

`You were like that once.` remarked Tony

`Was I? Must have been a long time ago, I don't remember.` Nigel sounded a little distant and surprised at Tony's comment.

`When you were her age... but it fades and when it's gone, it's gone forever. Other less important things begin to take over. That's the trouble. If we knew what a precious thing we had, when we had it then maybe we would try to hang on to it for a little longer. That's the price we pay for the journey from the innocence of youth. When I was Katie's age, I used to think I would live forever, nothing would affect me, but you lose that sense of immortality and you become weaker as you grow older, just when you really need to be growing stronger. Every temptation has to be paid for. I suppose the older, more experienced we become, the less impulsive, more cautious and suspicious we also become.

`So do we all become cynics as we grow old?` asked Nigel casually.

Tony laughed, `cynical, pragmatic and boring, that's what we become.`

`I don't think you're boring or cynical and there's nothing wrong with pragmatism.`

Tony smiled again, `that's because you're becoming one of us.`

`Us?` said Nigel wondering who the "us" was he was referring to.

`Old.`

`Oh, I see ......` said Nigel a little despondently.

`Did you love her?` asked Tony.

`Who?` said Nigel now unsure who Tony was referring to.

`Carla,` replied Tony.

Nigel thought for a moment about what he had been asked. It was unusual for Tony when talking to his children to refer to Carla by her Christian name even though they were divorced. The change of reference caught him a little off guard.

`Probably, but does it really matter. Would it make any difference now?`

`So you didn't? replied Tony.

`No I'm not saying that. I did love her of course I did. She was my mother after all is said and done, but a lot of time has passed and now I just don't know anymore. In a few years I'll look back, when this is all over, when it's all just a distant memory, maybe then I'll know, I'll be able to be more objective, but not now. It's much too early.

`She did love you all,` replied Tony, sounding uncharacteristically supportive. At times, even he may have had some doubts over the veracity and reliability of all the words on which he had based his assumptions. The nature of truth is that there is always a small element of untruth and with all lies there is undoubtedly some element of truth and this is what makes defining either a black art. Absolutely nobody can know the whole truth or tell a perfect lie; the paradox is that each depends on the presence of the other to truly exist.

`We never noticed,` replied Nigel abruptly. For some reason he resented the declaration, as if it seemed to have the potency to undermine and weaken the clearly defined opinion that he had shaped and held in his mind for so long about his mother. He wasn't prepared to simply allow that to be dispelled, nor simply deconstructed, not just yet if ever.. `

`I wasn't sure in the beginning,` added Tony a little hesitantly. He had obviously sensed Nigel's reluctance to forgive or absolve his mother of anything at that particular moment, but at the same time, he was also aware of something being brought to a closure. For this to be complete he would need to except that he too wasn't completely without fault or culpability.

`She wasn't an easy person to understand you know...` continued Tony listlessly, `as she grew older this impenetrable barrier slowly began to descend around her - to protect her from herself I suppose... For years after that I could never tell, what she was thinking or feeling, but then around the time that Katie was born I could suddenly see this barrier began to lift. It was as if a new chapter in her life had begun. She did come to love you all again... in the end.`

`Do you really believe that?` asked Nigel, not in a disbelieving way but more in genuine surprise as if he were actually glad to hear the words.

`Yes I think she did,` said Tony. `Before I left she had started to change, she was not so.... defensive, I don't know if it was because she was just getting older or whether she had come to terms with what had happened in the past. I suppose we all mellow with age, but at last, she had found a way to show some feeling, affection I suppose you could call it, towards all of you, even me, but by then it was too late. The damage was done, everything I'd felt for her was long dead, killed by years of cold indifference, but I'm sure she loved you, well, before I left I thought so, I couldn't have left if I didn't feel that.`

`But that was what over fifteen years ago. I had my own children by then. Bit late for a mother's love. I needed it when I was five, not twenty-five.` replied Nigel unsympathetically.

`I'm sorry about that,` said Tony apologetically, `but.. `

`Why do you do that dad?` Interrupted Nigel tersely, but without any real intent.

`What?` asked Tony innocently.

`Defend her... despite everything that happened. She didn't love you and yet you stayed. I will never understand why you didn't leave long before you did, there was nothing to hold you, she treated you appallingly.`

`We were married,` replied Tony. The reply was loaded with the onus of responsibility, a sense of obligation and commitment, but devoid of emotion.

`But what does that really mean if she didn't love you?`

`I loved her and she was still your mother,` said Tony.

`Only by birth. I had no other option, you did,` replied Nigel glibly trying to be a little clever with the words but not really making a point.

`I know she felt guilt, every day I could see that. She never stopped punishing herself for outliving her first child. Only a mother can really know what it feels like to lose someone so young, somebody you have carried in your body as part of you for nine months, somebody that is totally dependent on you for life for its very existence, suddenly taken without a moment's notice, no explanation and then being left alone.' Tony paused for a moment recalling something from the past.. `I remember I came home early once, just a few months after we had been married. I could hear her talking to someone upstairs in the bedroom. I wasn't sure who it was so I quietly made my way up and as I got towards the top of staircase I could just see into our bedroom and Carla was kneeling on the floor talking, no not talking, she was raging, raging at the sky. 'Why me God? why me? what have I done?' But there's never an answer. I should have gone into her, but I didn't. I crept back downstairs, left the house and came back later. That was my mistake not comforting her when she needed me. Only Carla knew how it felt to give all that love to one person and then suddenly find that person not to be there anymore. I often wondered what happens to the love. What happened to all that love she once had for Caroline, where did it go?`

Chapter 7

Sarah pulled into the half-empty car park and picked an empty spot as close to the office as possible. She locked the car door and walked casually to the main reception building enjoying the gentle warmth of the late summer sun. She had once made a promise to herself when she was much younger and unacquainted with the querulous nature of climate, that when it was her turn to be married it would be on one of these beautiful days.

She had been to a friend's weddings in April when it had rained and another friend's wedding when it was bitterly cold in October and she definitely didn't want that for the most important day of her life, yet to come. She understood there were never any guarantees with the weather, just like life, but the percentage bet had to be around August.

The girl behind the desk recognised her at once, smiled, made a passing comment of no consequence and wrote something down on a notepad. Sarah sat down, but no sooner had she done so, the receptionist waved her through to the room on the other side of the waiting room. Sarah always approached these meetings with a small degree of trepidation, not for any particular reason apart from the occasional unexpected disclosure, but she had become used to that. Nothing was ever completely unexpected.

`Come in Sarah take a seat.` Sarah moved across the room and sat in the only other chair in the room which faced the window and which due to its position partially precluded her from looking directly at the person in the chair behind the desk. But she knew the format by now and did not try to make any adjustment to the arrangement.

She looked at the jacaranda trees just outside the window, which had been blooming for over a couple of months now. She had always found the unique luminescent colour one of the most soothing she had ever seen. The lilac hue touched a sensor in her brain, which triggered a chill, relax - take it easy instruction in her sensory cortex. She wondered whether this was actually part of the treatment and if the doctor new about the tree and the affect the colour had or whether it was just plain serendipity. Accident or intuitive design it didn't really matter, it worked for her.

`So how are you feeling today?` asked Charlene her soft French - Canadian tone engendering a calm inspirational confidence, which was probably the most important part of her manner as far as Sarah was concerned. If you were unable to quickly place patients at their ease then all the qualifications in the world were of no real value and a complete waste of time.

`I'm fine thank you,` replied Sarah, `really good actually,` she added smiling at Charlene. She felt so quickly at ease once she was sitting down in the room that she could only liken it to a priests confessional, absolute discretion, no judgement no condemnation, even a sense of forgiving. This was in complete contrast to her sense of foreboding and reluctance prior to attending the first session, something she was now able to control and manage as she became more confident.

`Excellent,` replied Charlene. She paused for a few seconds just in case Sarah decided to continue. She knew the priceless value of silence and the physiological burden to fill a void and equalise the pressure of the vacuum. There were days when she would speak no more than a few words, but the dialogue could continue for a full hour.

`Any recollections after last week?` asked Charlene.

`Yes a few memories after I left, things I don't ever remember happening...` she paused while attempting to bring the memories back to mind, `I suppose they must of, but I'm just not entirely sure, it's almost as if I'm doubting their veracity, I kept asking myself whether maybe they happened to somebody else not me at all.'

'Why do you distrust your memory?' asked Charlene sounding intrigued.

Sarah paused for moment collecting her thoughts... 'I suppose it's because... because I have no previous recollection of the events, before our last session that is? But on that basis I suppose we would not believe any memories we have, which would mean nothing is real and that would be totally illogical.'

'Yes it would,' replied Charlene, 'maybe I just simply jogged your memory?'

Sarah looked over to where Charlene was sitting, but she could only see a shadowy outline, the greyed out figure of her tame inquisitor. 'Or is it just my imagination playing games, that's what I am unsure of?'

'That's normal at this stage. I can assure you they are true memories. I have never...' she paused momentarily, disturbed by her careless use of the word, as she had in fact once experienced an advanced case of dissociative personality disorder, classic schizophrenia and the patient had created complex fake memories under hypnosis which had fooled her completely... '...never had a patient who could fabricate events while under....'

'Your spell,' interrupted Sarah playfully.

'No not a spell,' replied Charlene, smiling at Sarah's remark.

'How do you know?' asked Sarah.

'How do I know what?' replied Charlene.

'How do you know someone is not just making it all up, trying to confuse you?'

'For what reason?' asked Charlene.

'I don't know I just wondered.'

'I would know,' replied Charlene with an air of professional confidence and adroit acuity which belied her normally easy going unchallenging style. There was a sense of unspoken mutual respect. Both of them immediately understood this. Sarah would have many doubts on this

84

journey, but Charlene would always be there to dismantle each concern as it arose.

'You see..,` said Charlene choosing her words carefully, 'What is happening is the more we delve into your past and the more we reveal from the earlier periods, the less your mind will suppress the unpleasant memories. But there is a price to pay for the truth and that is clarity of mind, which in a way is also a curse. We will find the answer and you will have to confront those issues that have lain hidden away for so long. It will be as if they were in a box, a memory box and all we are doing is slowly opening that box.

'To face my demons?` asked Sarah.

'Yes, you could put it like that.`

'A bit like Pandora?` asked Sarah with a hint of tenuous exuberance.

'No hopefully not quite as bad as that,` replied Charlene smiling reassuringly 'Just accessing the truth and from that you have nothing to fear.` But Charlene didn't know that for sure.

'So are you ready?`

'Yes.`

'Good well come on through and lay down on the couch as before.` Sarah followed Charlene into the adjoining room and took her position on the couch resting her head on a small pillow.. Charlene sat in the chair next to the couch and waited for Sarah to make herself comfortable. The heavy drape curtains were drawn and the lights had already been suitably dimmed.

'Now I want you to close your eyes and just relax forget about everything and relax. She waited a few moments. Now starting from your feet I want you to let all the tension go, very slowly relax, let the tension just fade away from every muscle, every tendon. You can feel all the tension slowly leave your feet, they are completely relaxed. You can hardly feel them now, they feel as light as a feather... she waited. Now your legs... just let all the tension fade away...

let them relax until they no longer have any weight and you cannot feel them anymore...` she waited again for a few moments before continuing, her somnolent tone gently exsanguinating her body of all angst and torment. Large passages of recent past elided into passing moments that seemed to fall away from body, excoriated layers now rendered redundant by exposure.

`Now your body.., just let all the tension go... let your body just sink into the couch and relax... now your arms, let all tension drain away and just relax.. and so she continued until Sarah was virtually asleep but she was not.`

`Are you feeling completely relaxed now?`

`Yes I am,` replied Sarah.

`Right now keep listening to my voice...I will be with you all the way..' she paused for a few moments, 'I need you to imagine a large empty room and in the middle of the room there is a staircase leading down to another room... now I want you to walk over to the staircase and walk down that staircase to the next room.. ` Charlene waited for a few moments before continuing.

`Are you there yet?` asked Charlene.

`Yes.` Sarah answered quietly.

`Good. Now in corner of the room there is another staircase, can you see it?`

`Yes,` Sarah replied.

`Good. Now this one takes you down to another large room and in the middle of the room is a chair. I need you to carefully walk down the staircase into the next room.` She waited...

`Are you there yet?`

`Yes I'm there.`

`Good. Can you see the chair?`

`Yes, yes I can.`

`Good. Now can you walk across to the chair and sit down.` Sarah didn't reply.

Charlene referred to the notes she had taken previously. She had detected a sense of despair in previous meetings, which she believed might have been the nucleus from which was created an environment within which they had formed their own unique relationship as a substitute for the maternal love that they were being denied. As far as she could determine from previous meetings, it started when Harry was eight and Sarah was five years old and lasted for a number of years. The innocence of their childhood had shrouded their personal awareness of the significance of their relationship, but the traumatic transition through to adulthood and the emergent awareness of the emotional implications of the childhood relationship may have affected them as they struggled to find some rational for what they had felt.

'Now I want to take you further back than last week, before you were seven years old. This time I want you to try to go back to a period before you were five years old, can you do that?'

'Yes I will try.' replied Sarah, she waited for a few moments.

It is late in the evening in the bedroom of a four-year-old girl who is sleeping. A small shaft of light, from a lamppost in the road outside, squints through the curtains and casts a sliver of silver across the bare wooden floor. A seven year old boy carefully and very quietly opens the bedroom door and enters her bedroom; he looks at the girl as she gently sleeps hardly making a sound and he moves quietly towards her bed. She slowly begins to wake aware that someone is in the room and she turns to look at the boy. She rubs her eyes and smiles with acquiescent approval. He smiles back at her and puts his finger to his lips and quietly mouths 'schhh' she smiles again, she is now part of the conspiracy. The boy moves closer and begins to nervously suck the end of his forefinger. They have not said a word, but they are reading each other's thoughts. He pulls back the blanket and then the sheet just enough to allow him to slip in beside the girl. Faintly in the distance emanating from the lounge below, where his father keeps the stereo system, he can hear Al

Martino singing `Here In My Heart` in the background. He can also just make out mumbled conversation, but he can't understand what they were saying. The heavy rain beats on the window and somewhere outside in the street a bottle falls over. For a few seconds they both lay perfectly still unsure as to what should happen next, the moment of hesitation passes they are together at last.

`Can you tell me where you are?` asked Charlene, her voice suspended in mid-air, sequestered from mortal existence in an illusion partly created by the parsimonious use of lighting and capricious intonation, is strangely soothing.

`I'm in my bedroom, it's my bedtime.` replied Sarah.

`Can you tell me how old you are?`

`I'm not sure, I think I am nearly five.` Charlene made a note on her pad, but not for any specific reason as the tape machine was recording every detail. In another part of the house, a clock softly chimed twice with a sound like tiny bells.

`That's a pretty sound,` said Sarah, she smiled with a decanted felicity that appeared to shroud a deeper emotional recollection which Charlene presumed must have been from a later period in her life. Once again she made a note on her pad as the precise inflection and cadence of Sarah's comment would not be accurately captured on the tape, but was never the less an important detail which she would return to at some later date.

`It's a clock, my mother gave it to me on my twenty first birthday.`

`That was nice,` replied Sarah.

`Yes I thought so.` Charlene waited for a few seconds and made a mental note to move the clock out of earshot.

`Can you tell me what you see?....`

`It's not very clear,` replied Sarah.

`Just relax and think of yourself when you were five years old,` she paused, 'can you remember your birthday a very special day. Your mother and father would have bought you some presents. Now can you see anything?`

`The door. I can see the bedroom door.`

`That's good now can you go into the bedroom and tell me what you can see?`

`I can see the window. I remember the pretty curtains.`

`What colour are they? `

`It's hard to tell but... yellow. I think the curtains are yellow. Yes, they are bright yellow with little pink flowers. I like yellow. Yellow is my favourite colour. Yellow is nice.` Sarah had begun to speak with a childlike inflection. Charlene had experienced this peculiarity before, but not often.

`Good. Now can you see anything else is in the room?`

`A box... a large box in the corner.`

Charlene made a note then continued.. `Is that a birthday present?`

`No, I've had it for ages...`

`Can you see what's in the box?`

`No I can't it's closed.`

`What colour is the box?`

`Yellow it's yellow,` She smiled. Charlene made a further note that presumably the box or possibly the colour bought back some happy memories for her.

`Can you walk over to the box?` Charlene paused for a moment to allow her time to cross the room in her mind.

`Are you there yet?`

`Yes, yes I am,` replied Sarah, sounding oddly reluctant.

`Can you open the box Sarah?`

Sarah became a little hesitant. `The lid is very heavy,` she replied, but her tone conveyed more about her unwillingness to open the box, than simply the weight of lid.

Charlene noted this listlessness and waited in silence for a few moments before continuing to press her a little further...

`Have you managed to open it?`

`Yes, yes I have.` Sarah's expression changed, no longer at peace, she clearly knew what was inside and it obviously concerned her because she had become visibly agitated.

`What's inside Sarah? There's nothing to worry about, I am here, with you, all the time.`

Sarah didn't say anything for a while so Charlene repeated the question. `Can you see what's inside the box Sarah?`

`Harry, Harry's inside, he's hiding.`

`Who's Harry?` asked Charlene, she knew who Harry was from previous sessions, but she still needed Sarah to confirm his identity.

`Harry's my brother silly!` replied Sarah huffily. She seemed to settle back down.

`Who is Harry hiding from?`

`I'm not sure; I think it's daddy, yes he's hiding from daddy.`

`Why is Harry hiding Sarah?`

`I don't know, but he likes to hide in the box sometimes.`

`Does he say anything to you?`

`He's sorry - and he's crying and he's scared.` replied Sarah, still sounding like a child.

`Why is he scared Sarah?` probed Charlene, sensing something relevant could be about to be revealed. Possibly something that could explain many things.

`He won't tell me. He says it is very bad. That's why he's crying. He wants me to close the box so he can sleep.` Sarah was becoming increasingly disturbed again by this and Charlene thought it would be best to stop at this point.

`Can you close the box for me, Harry will go to sleep and everything will be fine.` ...she paused for a few seconds.

90

`Have you closed the box Sarah?`

`Yes it's closed now.`

`Harry will be all right now won't he?` asked Sarah.

`Yes he will, he's safe in the box.` replied Sarah

`Does anybody else come into your room?`

`My daddy comes in sometimes, to tuck me in when it's time to go to sleep and he kisses me goodnight.`

`Does anybody else come in?`

`Mummy sometimes, but not much.`

`Is that all?`

`Yes I think so. I can't remember. I want a drink of water.`

`Are you going to fetch the water?`

`Yes... no... somebody brings me the water.`

`Who brings the water Sarah?`

`I don't know I can't see very clearly, it's very dark.... no it's.......Harry... my big brother Harry.` She smiles.

`Does he always bring you water?`

`Sometimes and sometimes we just talk.` replied Sarah.

`What do you talk about?`

`Being happy?`

`And are you?` Charlene asks.

`I don't know, I think so, but I will have to ask Harry.`

`Why do you have to ask Harry?`

`I always ask Harry,` replied Sarah, as if this was a natural presumption.

`Well ask him?` said Charlene.

`Do you want me to be happy Harry?` asked Sarah. The words hung in the air for a few moments and Charlene wondered what might happen next. Strangely, Sarah answered in a different voice, sounding more like a boy.

`Yes of course I do, always... I would have to die if I ever made you sad.` Charlene found that rather chilling, she felt the hairs on the back of her neck begin to prickle. This was the first time that Sarah had ever given any indication of the existence of a second personality and although Charlene initially put this down to a transitory vocal necessity to convey a recollection, it was still very unusual to adopt a different voice to convey that detail.

`Then I'm happy,` said Sarah.

`Why are you happy?` Charlene asks.

`Because Harry wants me to be... silly,` replied Sarah.

`Does Harry say anything else to you?`

`I can't remember anymore ...I'm feeling very sleepy.`

`OK, I think we'll finish now. That will be enough for today... Now I'm going to count slowly to five and then I am going to leave the room. When I get to five I want you to slowly wake up. Take your time, as you will feel very weak at first. When you sit up wait for a few minutes before you try to stand. When you are ready come into the other room. Are you ready?`

`Yes.` she replied.

`One,.. Two.... Three... Four... Five` as she counted Charlene slowly withdrew from the consulting room. As Sarah awoke she did feel very weak as Charlene had predicted and she just laid on the couch for about five minutes thinking back over what had happened. As she became stronger she sat up took a few deep breaths and then she stood up and walked slowly through the door into the adjoining room.

`Are you OK?` Charlene asked. She was sitting at a desk making notes.

`Yes. I'm fine thank you.`

`Please sit down.` she indicated the chair facing the Jacaranda trees.

'So what did we talk about today?' Sarah enquired cautiously.

'Harry and a box.' Charlene replied, carefully gauging Sarah's reaction. 'You spoke about being happy and how he wouldn't want to make you sad.'

'Harry is my brother.' replied Sarah sounding surprised.

'Yes you mentioned that.'

'What was the box?' asked Sarah.

'I think it what a toy box you had in your bedroom and Harry used to hide in it.'

'I don't remember a box.'

'It may come back to you in a day or two.'

'So why did Harry hide in it?' said Sarah a little confused.

'I'm not sure but I think it may be important, we may find out next time.'

'So did this help?' enquired Sarah.

'Yes I think it did. I think we are getting closer to the time when something happened, next time we will go back maybe a little further and find out more about why Harry hid in the box.'

'I will try to remember.' said Sarah

'No don't try to remember your mind has hidden this period for a reason and it will resist attempts to allow you to remember until we know more. Once we have found the reason we can discuss it and you will be able to rationalise it your mind and then you will find you can remember much clearer. Anyway I will see you next week the same time. Is that OK?

'Yes that's fine, thank you,' said Sarah, 'goodbye.' She left the room thinking about Charlene's words.

Chapter 8

Doctor James Clutterbuck entered Harry's room without knocking and glanced momentarily at Harry with the self-assured emotional detachment of someone who resided permanently on an elevated plateau of egotistical superiority. A grand table at which many of his contemporaries would one day hope to dine, but sadly few would ever receive an invitation. And yet he managed to accomplish this mystical aura of libertarianism without the slightest hint of arrogance. The trick, and it is a trick can only be accomplished by those who have been permanently anaesthetised against the realms of reality in which they have to exist and the relentless unforgiving nature of their work. He looked at Harry while slowly scratching his left ear with the forefinger of his left hand while the right hand remained firmly planted in his trouser pocket. He seemed to be leaning back slightly. This posture was pure thespianism almost histrionic, simply for visual effect and was obviously part of an elaborate routine enacted for all new patients. It was probably an idiosyncratic gesture purloined from one of his senior tutors, which he had found particularly interesting and suitably charismatic and which he had quietly tucked it away in his 'future persona box' to be recycled and rolled out for use at some later stage in his career which was now. For obvious reasons he would try out the new images on patients first (people who did not know him well) before weaving them into his normal façade. Somewhat erroneously he assumed that it exuded a degree of gravitas, which he thought to be attractive and which he now believed enhanced his profile amongst the medical community. However he was wrong, for he knew little about the intricate inner machinations and the psyche of hospital personal.

Their case hardened epithelium protected a thread of commonality that wove its inexorable path deep into the body and souls of all of those who laboured here. This was their slender lifeline to sanity and they each held on to it very tightly. To let go would render them lost forever in a diaphanous void of reality, destined to drift into eternity like an astronaut cut free from his umbilical cord. Forever battered by emotion and sentiment. Their objectivity lost forever.

James moved authoritatively towards Harry's bed, stood at the bottom and having finished scratching his ear, picked up the notes that were hanging on the end and began to read.

Harry carefully watched and observed James's slightly eccentric mannerisms out of the corner of his eye, but not so it was obvious. He said nothing for nothing had been said and for some reason he assumed possibly rightly or wrongly that any conversation should, by accepted protocol, be initiated by the doctor.

James had encountered many failed suicides over the years and had still not really come to terms with the concept. For him life was a relatively conventional "social template". His parents who were professional middle class and lived in the country just outside of Canterbury. His father was a local GP, his mother a Headmistress (but not at his school thankfully). He had attended a private boys school, an innocuous unchallenging period as far as he was concerned and apart from one particularly embarrassing episode when he found himself uncontrollably attracted to one of the sixth form boys for a whole term before his passion was brutally crushed by the sudden realisation that the sixth former in question was having a strictly heterosexual clandestine affair with the English tutor, who was summarily dismissed and the end of term. Generally, he had enjoyed himself at school and having acquired the requisite exam grades, transferred to university and then medical school. He met Marianne - who came from Bordeaux, but had lived in England since she was thirteen - at University and they had married exactly one year after he qualified.

They didn't fall in love immediately in fact it wasn't until nearly two years after they met when they were on a holiday in France at Marianne's Uncle's house in The Lot that he suddenly realised that he loved her very much and proceeded to profess his undying love for her at every possible occasion which at times had become a little embarrassing for her uncle who was - despite being a French centrist, which in itself was a non sequitur position bearing in mind France's political history, a nation always swayed either to the extreme left or right - made of sterner things and strangely, for a Frenchman, not overly keen on public displays of physical emotion. Marianne had begun to wonder whether the locally produced Merlot for which James had acquired a taste and of which he had consumed a not inconsiderable amount during the holiday, had some hidden ingredient, which had opened up an as yet untapped area of the brain, which controlled emotion. It was probably something to do with the truffles and mushrooms that grew prolifically in this region. Maybe they had inadvertently deposited a spore or some other as yet undetected pharmacological element into the ground that had found its way back into the grape. Marianne's uncle also drank the same chateaux but it did not affect him in the same way as far as she was aware. Oddly he committed suicide a few years later for no apparent reason.

Up to that point in their relationship it had been, what he believed was a purely sexual arrangement with sundry domestic benefits. That all changed during the holiday and had remained that way ever since. He reasoned that this was probably a dimension of the 'model' that he hadn't anticipated, but was never-the-less very happy with the development and looked forward to the next stage which would be four children, two boys and two girls, a large Georgian country house like his parents and a pair of Labradors, possibly Golden Retrievers.

Marianne had decided to continue in medical research and was working at the university. During the whole of this academic period from about the age of nineteen, suicides had been an interesting and sometimes impassioned subject for fellow student discussion in wine bars and pubs and at dinner parties. James's views, based loosely on a theory that most suicide victims were pre-programmed even preordained at birth, possibly before birth, with some form of manic depression gene and therefore no amount of therapy would ever deter them from their final objective, as this was their destiny. This jarred badly with and was always seriously derided by the opposing faction including Marianne who firmly believed it was in fact a manifestation of deep seated physiological problems probably related to experiences from a very early age that had disturbed the delicate equilibrium of the mind. Once tilted in one direction - *a little like Marianne's uncle* - and unless the in-balance was redressed, the outcome became inevitable. Either way they died and therefore it was just a matter of academic conjecture as to why. James had always had a deep mistrust for psychoanalysis, which he still firmly believed, was too imprecise to be reliable and to a large degree relied on the predisposition of the doctor as much as the patient. As far as he was concerned, it was a black art and under hypnosis, to a large degree, most people would say virtually anything as long as they had been carefully tutored beforehand. Most of what they said was piffle anyway as far as he was concerned. Furthermore, he firmly believed that a cosy heart to heart in the pub over a couple of pints would, in most cases, get to the bottom of all "personal" problems. Alcohol unquestionably succours the liberation of all inhibitions and promotes discussion of even the darkest of secrets.

His chosen discipline however relied on the clinical diagnosis of a disease or ailment by the intuitive interpretation of all the physical and biological evidence and the prognosis was therefore devoid of ambiguity. Never vague and hopefully seldom wrong. For James it was black and white and the demarcation lines were clearly defined. If you were overweight, you would eventually die from heart failure. If you had cancer you would almost certainly die from it unless you cut it out and you would still probably die from it (statistically that is). If you broke a leg you would not be able to walk until it was mended, it was as simple as that.

All the hocus-pocus with the psycho boys was just nonsense as far as he was concerned. In his damming opinion, psycho analysts could usually be relied upon to construct meaningful yet spurious reasons to effectively excuse almost anybody from excepting any tangible responsibility for almost anything they had done wrong in their lives. Not surprisingly, the basis of their defence would rely to a large degree on something as specious and inconsequential as the victim being deprived of a plastic dummy for five minutes, once, when they were three years old. He blamed the moral breakdown and the feral nature of society on the softly, softly approach taken by judiciary which had been unduly influenced by social workers who were effectively untrained psychiatrists and by definition the most dangerous of all because they had answers for everything, when they never truly understood the questions.

`Morning.... Harry, do you mind if I call you Harry?` asked James. He had now completed his review of the brief case notes. Harry did not hear him as he still had his earphones in place, but on seeing the doctor's lips move, he removed the earphones.

`Sorry? I missed that,` replied Harry politely but with casual indifference.

`I said good morning I'm your doctor.`

`Oh right, morning doc sorry I had the...` replied Harry apologetically, he pointed to the earphones.

`How are you feeling now?`

`How do you expect me to feel?` replied Harry a little inquisitively and with a dimension of aggression which was not really in his nature. He obviously still felt very disappointed at the failure of his primary mission.

`Hopefully better than yesterday,` said James sensing a reluctance to answer his question.

`Well I'm sorry to disappoint you, but I don't.`

James looked at the notes again to give himself time to consider whether a slightly blunter approach might be more advisable. Past experience had taught him it was important to pitch a conversation at the right level if you wanted to interact with a patient. Not to aloof and not to friendly, it was harder to convey bad news if you had become too friendly with them, but by the same token you needed to empathise with them which was not easy and could appear to lack emotional credibility and sincerity if you were completely detached. He decided to disregard the general advice advocated by the hospital management on bedside etiquette and try his hand at a personalised bespoke approach.

`Well you slashed your wrists, dumped four pints of blood between home, wherever that is and A & E and ingested enough ketamine to kill a herd of wild elephants. So that's to be expected. To be honest I'm surprised you're still here at all,` replied James a little acerbically, `…we didn't have a lot to go on when you arrived, the guy that dropped you off disappeared very quickly without telling us anything accept that you were unconscious and bleeding to death and we'd sort of worked that one out for ourselves.`

`Probably my dealer,` said Harry, `he does have a cracking after care service. Envy of the Western world.`

`Not that good if he nearly killed you. I thought the trick was to keep the customer alive.`

`He didn't try to kill, me that was self-inflicted.`

`Yep sort of worked that one out to,` replied James drolly.

`I don't know why you bother,` asked Harry, `still I suppose it's a few more brownie points for you.`

`That's what we do, save people from dying, when we can that is. It's very rewarding,` replied James now beginning to sound a little arrogant.

`To be honest I'm not sure I want to be,` replied Harry.

`Want to be what,` enquired James.

`Saved,` replied Harry brusquely.

'Why?' said James after some hesitation.

'Why? Not much to say really. I went for the emergency exit, you shut the door before I got there, ergo I failed.' Harry smiled at James, which James found a little disturbing. Visions of Jack Nicholson sprang to mind.

'No what I meant was, why did you try?' James was suddenly aware that he was drifting dangerously close to the discipline he most despised...

'I've had enough. I woke up yesterday morning and realised that it's all just a complete waste of time, so why bother any more. I mean is it actually worth keeping me alive, do I deserve that? For all you know I could be a child killer or a paedophile,' replied Harry.

'You could be, but it's not our job to judge and anyway that's not very likely statistically speaking and it wouldn't make any difference anyway. We save the good the bad and the stupid it's a non-partisan occupation; we don't have the luxury of meritorious selection.' Was he beginning to sound a little too arrogant he wondered.

'But why save me, if I don't want to be saved. Had you thought about that? Maybe I just don't want to deal with all this pointless triviality. I mean what's it all for really. Life is too short, often painful, extremely tedious, complicated well in my case it is and very boring most of the time and if by some stroke of luck I did manage to hang around long enough to sort it all out, I'm still going to wake up one day to find I've grown old and useless and totally dependent on somebody else to clean my arse as I slowly descend into a state of advanced gaganess.'

'The trick is to try to do something worthwhile in between, then you find you don't have the time for self-pity and remorse,' replied James almost ecclesiastically.

'You're beginning to sound a bit like God or one of his preacher men and that's a little worrying,' replied Harry. 'Please tell me you're not a witness,' pleaded Harry

'Witness,' enquired James unfamiliar with the term.

`Jehovah's..` explained Harry.

`Ah no, but it's a shame you aren't, as we couldn't have given you any blood and you would have died, but you're not and we did and you aren't,` replied James.

`So I've noticed,` replied Harry now looking a little disappointed with an overriding sense of a loss of finality.

`As I was saying,` continued James, `You have to do something with your life then maybe you wouldn't feel this way.`

`Easy for you to say, but then yours probably wasn't screwed from the start, your life will always be better than mine and yours probably won't get fucked up and will be different, but most of the rest of us are condemned to serve out the sentence in a dungeon of boring indifference. From the moment we're born the whole thing is ingenuously mapped out in front of us. From the second we're dragged screaming from the bloody womb. If only we had the inner strength and stoic insight to face reality at an early stage and see all the shit ahead, then maybe we wouldn't go any further and call it a day there and then before wasting any more time tumbling down some obscure back road to nowhere.`

`I'm not with you,` said James.

It's all a bit like a train journey you know?` said Harry tutorially

`I still don't follow,` queried James.

`Life, life is a train journey you see it starts out like a little fun ride at the seaside, it chugs along slowly at first admittedly, but it's a pace you can handle. A few ups and downs nothing to hectic, it stops a few times to let new friends on an old friends off and takes you to new places along the way but there is nothing much to worry about. The food trolley comes around quite regular and you have a bit of fun and stick your head out the window occasionally and smell the steam and the smoke and let the wind rush through your hair and it's all rather pleasant. Occasionally you might

101

hit a tight turn or come to an unexpected stop and sometimes you dive off on a small diversion, but eventually you come back to the main line and carry on until you're about seventeen or eighteen; and then maybe you move up to the university carriage and that carries on for another three uneventful years before you pull into the big station. Then you change trains, get off the little steam train and get on the big high-speed train and you leave the station for the big journey. Only then once you are on this train do you suddenly realise you're the driver and you don't know how exactly all the controls work, but despite this the train is moving faster and faster and you're whizzing through some stations without even stopping. When you do stop at a station some of the passengers who have been with you for a long time have to leave and more new ones and sometimes a few old ones get on and then off you go again even faster than before and all the time you still haven't worked out how the controls work and sometimes you go off on the wrong line and it takes a long time to find your way back to the main line and when you do get back you find you missed quite a lot of things, because you've been too busy trying to work the controls and find your way back you've ignored some of your first class passengers so they got off. And then one day somebody taps you on the shoulders and points out the window and you can see the end of the line and you start to slow down and pull into the station and jump off only too happy to get away from all the pressure of being the driver and you look back and nearly all the people who were with you at the start of the journey have gone and all the rest are strangers. So you wonder to yourself when did that happen and was it worth the journey and maybe I should have never got on the train in the first place? So what's the point? All I want to do is cut out all the travelling in between and get to straight the end, is that so bad?`

`Not when you put it like,` replied James thoughtfully. `It's pointless just to exist unless you make some kind of contribution. You have to bring something with you if you are invited to the party that's the rule. You can't just turn up, drink the wine, eat the food steal the furniture and bugger off. It was an odd analogy but Harry got the drift of it.

`But what if I did take something,' replied Harry, 'something I could never return, something so precious that you're only get it once and when it's gone that's it, game over. That's what I did, so there was never going to be a party for me. I just wanted to wipe the page clean, the only way I know how, a sort of final atonement if you like, but now you've screwed up my stab at salvation and any prospect of redemption I had is gone.`

`I didn't know that did I?' replied James.

`You mean being stoned, rat arsed and pissing pints of blood out of my wrists didn't give you a tiny clue that maybe things weren't exactly hunky dory?' replied Harry a little harshly with an expression of matter of fact bewilderment which less than subtly conveyed a tone of stunned incredulity, that from the available information it was not possible to formulate a reasonably accurate assessment of what was actually going on in his head.

`No. No it didn't. But even if I did, it still wouldn't make any difference to me. Nothing's that bad that it's worth dying for. There's only a few good things worth that much. Tell me something have you ever heard of Pascal's Wager?`

`No,' replied Harry slightly mystified. `Something to do with horseracing?` he ventured whimsically.

`No,' replied James, not sure whether Harry was being indolently capricious or just plain ignorant. `He was a French philosopher who formulated a theory, well more common sense really if you think about it, anyway his "theory," was that on balance it was probably better to believe in God than not just in case God did exist, that way you covered all the options statistically and nothing was lost.`

`There you go again preacher healer man talking about God,' mused Harry, a little softer than before realising he had been giving James a hard time without any real justification.

`Not God just life, I was paraphrasing his theory,` replied James a little despondently, he had spent a large part of his life learning how to keep people alive and meticulously absorb the psychological dimensions necessary to support and reinforce his vocation, but had never really given any thought to this diametrically opposed option. `I was just trying to make a point that it has to be  better to be alive and keep trying, than be dead and never have the opportunity does that not make sense?`

`Possibly,` replied Harry reluctantly.

`Anyway it could have been an accident for all we know. You might have been having a great time at a party somewhere, got a little drunk, popped a few pills when your wrists were suddenly and unexpectedly ravished by a demented man eating Hamster, then again you might just have been having an off day, it could happen to any of us,` said James light heartedly.  `I have those too.`

`I'm having an off life.` replied Harry abruptly. `Maybe I should stick a sign round me neck, This world is all a load of crap!  If found dying please don't revive.` Would that be better?`

`Eloquently put if a bit gloomy,` replied James sanguinely with a smile.

`Not my words somebody else who was pissed off.`

`We would still have to try,` said James.

`I thought you might,` replied Harry with a resigned acceptance.

`So have you really done something that terrible?` James, who was not one to give in easily decided to try a slightly different less subjective tack.

`I think so, could even be an original sin.`

`An original sin that would be unique?  He smiled to himself at the unintentional pun  `How do you know that?

Every act, every thought, every feeling you could possibly have, someone somewhere must have had before. There are too many people in the world for any original sin so all that's left is a rehash of somebody else's ingenious abomination. So whatever it is you've done, you're not the first and you definitely won't be the last. Whatever it is there has to be a redemption and you don't have to die to get it...`

`Now you sounding like a preacher again,` snapped Harry.

`I'm a good catholic and I'm trying to be a friend,` James replied. He could feel the defensive barriers lowering slightly and he was now more determined than ever to help if he could.

`From all our sins?` enquired Harry.

`Yes I think so,` replied James, with reassuring conviction.

`So who is this person who gives me this absolution? asked Harry. `I've haven't found him and I've been looking for a long time.`

`Everybody can forgive, will forgive you, whatever you've done, but you have to find your own salvation. Nobody else can do that for you.`

`So it's all comes back down to me really and you just pass the accountability buck,` replied Harry.

`That's where you find redemption in accepting what's been done and dealing with,` answered James.

`If I'm responsible for my own redemption than I must also be responsible for my own life?`

`You are, that's the whole point.`

`But I wanted to die and you stopped me.`

`Yes,` confirmed James cautiously, aware that he had left a door slightly open....

`You said I was responsible for my life and therefore my death so it has to be my choice, yes?` asked Harry, engendering some kind of confirmation.

`It is your choice, I agree, but if you fail and you did, we have to spend our time and resources to bring you back. We don't have a choice, you do. Maybe you should talk to a priest; he's probably better equipped to help you answer the question of morality.`

`I don't think a priest could help me now. I'm well past the soul saving stage.`

`Are you?` asked James.

`I think so` replied Harry.

`Are you going to try it again?` asked James pensively

`Sin?` asked Harry with mocking surprise at the directness. `I'll try not to,` deliberately evading the real question and sounding a little facetious into the bargain.

`Suicide,` replied James bluntly, clarifying his previous question.

`I don't know,` said Harry light heartedly. `But as you're responsible for me now, I don't feel as bad about it as I did. Might even be easier next time... knowing that.` he grinned at James almost mischievously.

`I'm not trying to make you feel good about it and I'm definitely not responsible for you.` replied James.

`But you are,` replied Harry contrarily. `You see from the moment you saved my life you took over all responsibility for it, you became accountable. I relinquished my obligation when I tried to kill myself and you accepted it when you saved me. Haven't you read your Arthurian legend or maybe it was the Koran?`

James didn't answer immediately, but instead considered how best to respond, when Harry continued..

`So now I'm your problem...`

`I don't care what you've read. I don't accept,` replied James defensively, but Harry had rather neatly and quite succinctly disassociated his metaphysical onus of responsibly and as far as he was concerned dumped it squarely back with James.

'You have to accept, you don't have an option; you're stuck with it. You're here, you're talking to me, helping me to get better, so you've already acknowledged part of the responsibility, so it's not my concern anymore. In fact I feel quite good about it, you've helped me a lot doc.` Harry smiled and looked at James possibly a little to smugly, but without any discernible arrogance, for just a moment he believed he had gained an intellectual advantage over someone who he now considered to be his philosophical sparring partner and this ironically had made him feel a little better than he did, when all the previous reassurances by James had not really had any effect.

'I don't have to play this stupid game,` said James who was now a little irate that he had unwittingly acceded to Harry's dubious, but never the less astute observation.

'It's not a game doc this is for real,` replied Harry with supercilious superiority. He was going to play the advantage rule for all it was worth.

'I can assure you it is, you're just playing around with the words to make them fit the situation, very articulate and adroit I admit, but that's all it is,` replied James already painfully aware before the words had even left his mouth that they were a poor rebuke and a sadly inefficient retort to James's clever verbal gymnastics. He was capable of better, but James had somehow disturbed his equilibrium and corrupted his normally rational and erudite thought process.

'Isn't life about juggling the words to fit the situation?` replied Harry? Playfully. 'I mean take the word "assure" that you used just now; that is a very disturbing word in itself. By definition, it confirms, reassures and should give comfort, but in the dark murky depths that lay below and behind the word, it paradoxically hints at doubt and distrust and even betrays itself. Why is it when a doctor assures you all is well you immediately assume instinctively that he is withholding something germane something life changing, or when a politician assures you he has told you everything he knows, you know intuitively that he is only telling you what he wants you to know, see what I mean? Now is that me playing with the words or are the words playing around with you?`

James was becoming further infuriated at not being able to deflate this cogent, fluent and ruthlessly eloquent argument and quickly losing patience decided to alter the course of the conversation to allow himself time to consider the question. For some reason the old Bonaparte adage about it being bad manners to interrupt an enemy who is about to make a catastrophic mistake came to mind, but on this occasion it was a case of not interrupting the opponent being the imperative, in order to stop himself from making a catastrophic mistake.

`Your mother's outside. I think she wants to talk to you, so I'd better not hold you up any longer, you should explain your theory to her.` James knew this was a desperately pitiable defensive tactic and worse, unfortunately, he also knew that James knew it as well.

`OK.` said Harry smiling at his vanquished foe deciding that being magnanimous was the better part of victory and now was a good time to tactfully withdraw.

`If you belong to anybody it's her, she gave birth to you so she's the one who gave you your life not me.`

`Yes she did,` agreed Harry quietly but almost scornfully, `but she was also the one who also took it away.`

`Took it away? Looks to me like you're the one doing that.`

Harry was going to reply but decided not to bother and just queried, `is she all dressed up?`

`Yes like she's going to a wedding,` answered James

`My sister's.`

`Your sister's? bit selfish killing yourself on your sister's wedding day?`

`I'm not dead, yet.` Harry reassured him. `You saved me, didn't you?`

`So we did,` replied James apologetically. `But why on her wedding day?`

`Why not? I wanted to make it a memorable occasion.`

`Well I think you definitely succeeded there.`

`Not really. I'm still here, I could even make it to the service at a push, but I needed to be dead for real impact.`

`Who are you trying to impress?` said James inquisitively still not sure where Harry was coming from.

`Not trying to impress anybody,` said Harry without any inflection.

`Yes you are, you're doing it for somebody but who, your mother, your sister?`

`It's for me I told you that.`

`It is your sister. Is she the one you're trying to impress?` James was beginning to form a theory in his mind and the catharsis for the his frustration could only be brought about when the centrifical mass of confusion circulating in his mind could be focused on the real problem which had to lie with Harry's mother or his sister. He reasoned that Harry's sister was the percentage bet.

`I don't hate my sister, I hate myself and in fact I love her very much.` James then knew instinctively he had called it right.

`If you love her why do you want to kill yourself on her wedding day?`

`I need to find peace...`

`By killing yourself! but it would ruin her wedding and it's such a nice sunny day.` He could afford a little lateral musing at this point.

`Ruin her wedding, I will be dead you know. I will miss it too.`

`That's your choice,` replied James.

`What happened to the caring responsible doctor I used to know?` said Harry defensively, deciding to tactfully withdraw to a defensive position from where it would be easier to deflect further searching questions.

`Ah, well you see  death does tend to have a curious effect on the way I arrange the priorities in my life, especially when I meet someone as selfish as you.`

`Your bedside manners definitely need a little work.`

`They do when I meet people like you wasting their lives and my time.`

`So where am I on your list now?` enquired Harry almost retrospectively.

`Bottom.`

`Bottom! But I'm your personal responsibility.  Surely I should be top.`

`I don't think so, life is a one-way journey and you're going the wrong way so until you decide to change direction I'm not interested in helping you save it.  I'll patch up your body if I have to,  but you have to mend the hole in your soul.`

`And that's it?`

`As far as I'm concerned it is.  I'll send your mum in.`

`Yes you do that,` replied Harry. James left the room and Harry resumed playing with the pencil.

Chapter 9
1973.

The boy who is now ten years old enters his sister's room (she is now seven years old.) As he enters the bedroom, a television can be heard downstairs. He closes the door behind him, walks over to the bed and touches the girl on the arm to wake her. She turns over, looks up at him with resigned acceptance and slowly sits up in bed. The boy starts to fiddle with his pyjamas and she moves toward him. They make no sound for fear of attracting their parent's attention, for although they have been doing this as far back as she can remember she knows that something is not quite right.

She has spoken to friends at school, but they make no mention of similar activities or the existence of sibling relationships that extended beyond the supposed emotional bonds of love, enmity and thoughtfulness. She has become cautious about mentioning what she and her brother do, the acts that they perform, for fear of drawing a non-sequitur. They now seem to live part of their lives in a chthonic actuality, a teething mass of confused thoughts and counter thoughts, into which they merge during the evening but separate again during the day. Harry never talks to her during the day about what happens and now it has become part of the inexorable evening routine. Sara has unwittingly become an accomplice in something she does not understand, something that is beyond all normal comprehension. She also feels a strange discarnate desire to belong, something that she cannot explain. Harry cannot stop as he craves the satisfaction and the intimacy of this relationship.

When they have finished Sarah gets got out of bed and walks down stairs. She enters the lounge where her mother is watching the television alone. Harry goes back to his bedroom.

'Mummy, Can I have a glass of water for Harry?' Carla continues to watch the television and does not look at Sarah.

'Where is he? Carla asks, wondering why Harry didn't come down.

Sarah hesitates. 'He's in bed, he asked me to get the water.'

'Tell him to get his own water from the bathroom upstairs.'

'He doesn't like to go into your bedroom. It's easier if I get it mummy.'

'Easier!' replies Carla with mild consternation, 'What does that mean?' she was strangely surprised by the odd use of the word.

'He gets angry if I don't do as he asks.'

'If he gets angry, you tell me and I'll have a word with him.'

'If you do that he will get even angrier. Please don't say anything mummy.'

Carla was finding the conversation tiresome, it was also interrupting the program she was watching. 'All right all right, I won't say anything. Go to bed.'

'Can I fetch the water?'

'Yes, yes, get the water.'

'Thank you mummy.' She walks through to the kitchen, fills a glass with water and goes back to her bedroom where she has a drink herself before taking the glass into Harry. He drinks the water and she goes back to her bedroom. Sarah gets into bed and goes back to sleep. Tonight will be almost forgotten tomorrow.

Chapter 10

`Mum must have known we wanted to love her and how much you loved her, that's what I don't understand. That's what I find so confusing?` There was a desperate sadness in Nigel's voice, heavy with an uncertainty. The palpable liquidity of wretchedness and sorrow sank to the floor and crept languidly into to every corner of the room, so tactile you could almost touch it, grasp it in your hand. The inevitable bitter recriminations that had begun to surface were a natural reaction to his mother's unexpected death and a desperate attempt to understand what had driven her to take her own life.

`Maybe we needed that, something to obscure the lucidity.` replied Nigel.

`What, confusion?` queried Tony, slightly puzzled.

`Maybe sometimes it's necessary...` he paused for a moment... `I think it was a 16th century cardinal who said, "If you remove all the ambiguity in the world, what you have left will always be to your detriment" Maybe it was something like this he was referring to.`

`So better not to know everything?` suggested Tony.

`Yes, some of the time... possibly. It seems to make sense in an odd sort of way.`

`She did know we loved her, but maybe that just wasn't enough.` replied Tony.

`Enough? Enough for what?` rounded Nigel, vicariously, the sense of rage and frustration burnt indelibly in to every syllable.

`To destroy the demons inside her...` replied Tony. `Was the love we had for her strong enough to outweigh the hurt and guilt she felt inside. That's what we'll never know, what it felt like for her, what she went through alone every day, always asking the same question, was it her? Was it something she did?`

`You did love her?` asked Nigel, almost as a valediction as if to reassure himself that she had taken something with her to her grave.

`Yes, yes I did once. I loved her very much, for a long time I loved her and sometimes I thought she loved me, but it's not always what it seems. One loves and one is loved isn't that the way it is? Maybe she just couldn't love anyone anymore. I don't know. Tony took another sip of the whiskey.

`You could have left?` suggested Nigel, more as explanation than instruction.

`Like her first husband did? Yes I could have walked away and caused her more pain, but did she deserve that? Or I could stay, say nothing, work at it and hope things got better. What I didn't realise, was the price I would have to pay, that a very small almost imperceptible part of me would die each day, until one day I woke up and realised there was nothing left. Every last trace of desire and longing, in fact every feeling I ever had for her had been slowly eaten away by years of emptiness and regret, indifference and eventually contempt. Worse still she had grown to despise me for staying, because she thought I was there out of pity and you should always be wary of the destructive nature of pity. It's the same if you can't forgive, it destroys you in the end, not the other person.

`You did stay for over twenty-five years, so was she right?` asked Nigel hesitantly.

`No, it wasn't out of pity that was the irony of it. Why should I? I didn't know what had happened, Sarah didn't tell me anything until she was nearly twenty-four and by then it was too late to do anything, it had all finished years before. The damage was already done, that was when I realised why Carla had been the way she was for so long. I thought she was still blaming herself for what happened to Caroline, but she was thinking about something else altogether. Maybe that's why she grew to despise me because I stayed and she had to face me every day; that was a constant reminder that there was no one else to blame, but that was the irony, nobody was really to blame. It was just the unfortunate combination of circumstances. If they had happened in any other order the outcome would probably have been completely different, but they didn't.` Tony took another sip of the whiskey.

`A lot of wasted years for you,` mumbled Nigel looking down into his cup.

`Not really. We all make sacrifices of one kind or another in this life. You can't get out for nout as my old dad used to say. Love is about giving as well as receiving, not necessarily in equal amounts and sometimes that means giving something up. In my case, time, but it was worth it. I saw you all grow up and I had all your love and I've had Kathy's love for the last twelve years. That's enough, I don't think I missed out on too much. I'm happy with that.`

`But she stole those years and gave you nothing back. You only get them once and now they've gone.`

`If she was a thief of time, I was her willing accomplice. Most of us spend large parts of our lives doing something we don't really want to do, but if you're with the person you want to be with, then that's the deal you have to take. For me that was Carla and she was all I wanted. Very few of us get to fulfil our dreams and ambitions without some kind of emotional trade off, the rest of us settle for something slightly less, not quite what we wanted, not quite what we'd hoped for, but it's good and it will do. Occasionally you think of what might have been, had you been dealt a different hand, but you accept what you're given, grudgingly maybe, but you do accept it. Living with someone, with anybody, has to include an element of compromise or we would all be living alone and then we'd all become very bitter and resentful.` Tony half smiled.

`You could still have left her years ago?`

`Son, what you have to understand is the rate of attrition was imperceptible, it was like being silently desensitised. I never really noticed what was happening until one day twenty-five years had passed by and we weren't in love anymore.` Tony stopped for a few moments and thought about what he had just said, he had never actually said the words before. There had never been anybody he wanted to explain it to, not until now.

`But there were some good times you know, great days - funny days, days when we were so in love that I couldn't imagine life without her. So it wasn't all bad, being there watching you and David being born, watching you all grow up, those were good years. I would have missed all of that had I left. I still think back to the summers when we all used to play cricket in the garden. Harry was about sixteen by then - you were about what eight or nine and David was six and Sarah just a teenager.`

Nigel interrupted. `I remember Harry smashed a ball into old Wainthropp's Greenhouse next door and broke loads of glass. We all hid in the shed for hours playing cards when Wainthropp came looking for us. He kept walking up and down his garden and wouldn't go back inside.`

`Carla told him we were all in the village doing some shopping,` added Tony smiling, `and he believed her even though he was holding the offending cricket ball which had my name on it. She told him I'd lost it ages ago and he still believed her, very convincing.`

`She was a good liar... even then.` Nigel could never completely let go of the resentment he felt.

`Sarah seemed OK today. It didn't affect her the way I thought it would,` remarked Tony, adroitly redirecting the conversation.

`Strangely she enjoys funerals, she always has,` remarked Nigel.

'I find it hard to believe that anybody likes being at a funeral,' replied Tony a little surprised at Nigel's observation.

'I think Sarah made a special effort for her mother,' replied Nigel almost sardonically.

'Does she still hate her,' asked Tony though he knew what the answer would be, but he had to ask anyway. Sarah seldom spoke about her mother to Tony directly and he chose not to go to places where there were still too many bad memories.

'She was betrayed dad, what do you think?'

'She was just an old lady who deserved some redemption at the end,' replied Tony almost defensively, maybe the memories of happier days had worn away the bitterness he felt and had managed to keep so carefully hidden for so long; and maybe it was time for a graceful valediction. Tony was not a man for harbouring resentment, an admirable trait he had inherited from his father, a man who had strong northern ways.

'She wasn't always old,' said Nigel who, surprisingly, didn't inherit the same magnanimous quality from his grandfather.

'I'm still very afraid for you all,' said Tony with a sense of trepidation the nuance of which lingered in the words as much as in the content.

'Why? She's gone. There's nothing left now but the memory and that will fade in time,' replied Nigel abruptly.

'That's the bit I'm afraid of, the memory. I can't do anything about that.'

'You don't have to. We are OK. This is closure for them and me. It ends today, or at least it starts to end.'

'Does it though?' asked Tony. 'I still think I was partly to blame. I still can't believe I never saw anything. I keep wondering if there was something I missed, a telling glance, a gesture, I don't know, something I should have seen, but maybe ignored. You miss so much just because you only see

117

what you want to see, even when it's right in front of you hidden in plain sight.`

`Dad you were nothing to do with it. You weren't even there for the first five years, that's when it all really started.`

`But why didn't it stop, when I married your mother. That's what I don't understand?` replied Tony, reproaching himself and sounding fearfully bewildered.

`Because nothing changed,` said Nigel `she allowed it to continue. She never loved Harry or Sarah and when you married her all they saw was that she appeared to be capable of loving somebody, just not them.`

`But I loved Harry and Sarah exactly the same as you and David. I never had a favourite or anything like that.`

'Maybe it was something to do with their father?' suggested Nigel, 'maybe she hated him so much she took it out on them I don't know.' Tony didn't answer.

Although he was obviously aware of the existence of Harry and Sarah's father, Barry had to all intent played no part in their lives since Tony and Carla had married. Apart that is from the occasional Christmas and birthday cards in the early years. Invariably the birthday cards arrived on the wrong day sometimes even the wrong month. Carla would hide the cards and produce them on the appropriate dates. Barry had never enquired after their wellbeing and they in turn had tacitly reciprocated by seldom mentioning him except in an oddly estranged third party context. It was almost as if a mutual agenda of exclusion existed, but something he was not a party to. Over the early years Tony had deliberated many times over this self-imposed denial and in the early days had often wondered what possible reasons their father might have had to make the a decision to sever all contact with them. But as the children grew older and the cards stopped arriving, he gave it less and less thought.

His first instinct was that Barry must have had the same natural feelings for his children as Tony now had for them and yet on the basis of the evidential lack of contact this obviously was not the case. This was something he couldn't comprehend with any degree of clarity, but ironically this refutation had made the formation of the paternal relationship that now existed between them, far easier than he had anticipated and he now truly felt in every respect that he was their father. When he was younger the concept had been alien to his conventional comprehension of lifestyle arrangements, but with each passing year his views had softened, mellowed, matured and changed, more so than he had thought possible. His love for all his children was equal to that which any man would profess for his children.

`We know you loved us, we always knew that, but for her that was the hardest thing of all. The one sense, the one emotion she couldn't handle.` replied Nigel.

`What me loving my children?` exclaimed Tony a little surprised and slightly bewildered by this declaration.

`No not you loving us...` replied Nigel, `it was Carla coming to terms with how you could love Sarah and Harry the same way as you loved us, even though you weren't their father. No matter how she tried, she couldn't do that. Carla couldn't understand that and I don't think she ever did. She may have even resented you for being able to love them... us.`

Tony began to see something he had never really considered before. Had he ever really stood back and looked at the relationship objectively instead of only considering how he had felt and still felt about all his children, which for him was very transparent and uninhibited, instead of considering how Carla had felt? Had he been too timid in the face of self-possession to see something that maybe had always been there, but he had sub consciously chosen to overlook and ignore. His love for Carla had always been very intense despite insignificantly rare, overt reciprocation and perhaps this had blinded him temporarily over the years. At times, he had even found this predilection to detachment, this ability to encapsulate her emotional relationships in different boxes, to be an attractive quality in Carla.

119

`Maybe you're right, but now we'll never know.`

`It doesn't matter anyway.` replied Nigel.

`Hadn't you better go back to bed, Barbara will be wondering where you are?` enquired Tony.

`It's OK She's fast asleep. Are you sure you don't want anything?` asked Nigel.

`No son, I have everything I want now…`

`Goodnight dad.`

`Goodnight Son.`

Nigel moved his head slightly to one side and ran his left forefinger slowly up and down the side of his neck, thinking over what they had said. `I love you dad.` He smiled as a son does to a father he loves.

`I love you to son.`

Nigel went back to bed and Tony resumed looking out of the window. The church bells rang out on a warm Saturday morning in July.

Chapter 11

Virtually   unnoticed for she had now become almost invisible, Carla wistfully negotiated her route down the corridor on her way to Harry's room. As she did, she passed James and she   smiled at him in that curious way that strangers half acknowledge each other when in close proximity never completely sure if it will be misinterpreted. An older woman and younger handsome man engaged in a brief token gesture could, she thought, be involved in a relationship not fleeting or contrite, but filled with obsession and passion the like of which she had only known once before. She quietly yearned once more for those brief all-embracing moments of pleasure she had experienced from her younger days, moments filled with desire that promised so much, but now nothing more than hazy distant memories. She shared these thoughts with no one.

Doctor Clutterbuck smiled back with the polite utilitarianism so skilfully crafted to instil a confidence and yet so sadly bereft of sincerity, that in a fraction of a second the delusion would fade and die. He did not notice the faint trace of alcohol lingering on her breath, which was almost completely obscured by the overwhelming pervasive hygienic tang that penetrated and suffused every molecule of air in the hospital. The guilt of iniquity laid heavy and deep only tempered by the solace of her bibulous existence.

Clutterbuck detested the sanitized hospital aroma.   It disorientated his sensibilities and invaded his brain but, better the stench of purification, than desensitisation by the prescient odour of blood, death and despair that would replace it. After he had passed by and the moment was gone, he turned back and seeing Carla   enter Harry's room he wondered who she might be.   Probably his mother he surmised and contemplated what iniquitous secrets from the past had brought them all together on this day. He could hear the church bells ringing far away in the distance, unbeknown to him another timely reminder of one more person playing their part as the events of the day gradually unfolded. He continued his rounds without further incidence, but never far from his thoughts was the unexpected seed of responsibly that Harry had so skilfully and precisely planted in his brain. Never before had he encountered or considered this concept and it would be some time before he would eventually came to terms with and rationalise his concerns.

'Hi,' said Harry greeting his mother spryly as if nothing had happened. Carla did not know exactly how to react and pensively made her way over to Harry's bed before replying. She kissed him on the brow and ran her hands through his hair.

'Hello Harry.' she said, smiling as she did so, before sitting down.

'You look beautiful Carla.' The nominative compliment sounded strange, coming from her son.

'Thank you,' she paused for a second, 'I prefer mum.'

'Ok, you look mum Carla.' He looked at her with a strange impish expression.

'That's not what I meant,' replied Carla smiling.

'I know what you meant mum, you look beautiful.' Harry smiled.

'That's sounds better,' said Carla. 'I'm going to Sarah's wedding, that's why I'm all dressed up.'

'She'll like that,' said Harry.

'Do you really think so?' replied Carla sounding a little unsure.

'Did she send you an invite?' asked Harry almost rhetorically.

'Yes she did,' replied Carla thoughtfully.

'There you go then. She wants you there,' said Harry comfortingly.

'But she would, wouldn't she,' said Carla, speaking in that guarded manner that shell shocked divorcee's speak, no longer able to put their trust in any man, even their own son. Independence, self-reliance, finely honed intuition, acute cynicism and a disinclination to take anything at face value, all now an intrinsic part of her personal defence mechanism.

'She wants you there mum, that's why she invited you.'

'I do hope so, I don't want to ruin anything else,' replied Carla.

'You didn't ruin anything and you won't, not now. It's all finished and we've all moved on, you didn't do anything wrong anyway,' replied Harry with encouraging authority. He picked up a glass of orange juice, took a sip and put the glass back down on the cabinet by the side of the bed. He glanced out of the window to where the sound of church bells could be heard gently ringing, it was somewhere far away in the distance, someone else's life, someone else's world.

'Didn't I?' said Carla gingerly, 'the problem is I don't really don't know that anymore, I don't know anything for certain anymore.'

Harry turned back to look again at Carla and suddenly for just a rare moment he caught sight of the vulnerable person beneath the makeup and realised how tired and old she looked, way beyond her sixty three years. Behind the makeup, he could see a sad hesitancy he had not seen before. It was as if part of her soul had gone and in its place was an automaton, reacting in a pre-programmed safety mode with a specific agenda not to cause offence. This was not the mother he knew, and the uncharacteristic lack of spontaneity and obsequious manner drained him quickly and gave him cause for concern. It was almost as if she was feeling what he was feeling but even more so and maybe she was.

'It was not your fault, it was nobody's fault,' exclaimed Harry firmly, as if a confessional act of contrition were necessary at that precise moment.

`That's nice of you to say, but that's not what everybody else thinks,` replied Carla.

`Well that's their problem let them deal with it,` said Harry defensively.

`It doesn't feel like their problem when I still feel guilty.`

`You know the truth, that's all that matters in the end,` said Harry.

`Is it I wonder,` said Carla, `did you know what you did was wrong?`

Harry could hear a radio somewhere quietly playing Santana's Samba Pa Ti, a song he had always loved. He shut his eyes and listened for a few seconds while carefully thinking about Carla's question.

`Did I know it was wrong?` repeated Harry quietly `No I didn't, but then I didn't know it was right either. I couldn't tell the difference, well not then and that rather muddied the water a bit, well for me it did. Even now I'm not sure about it, but everybody else seems to be, so I guess it was wrong and deep down I suppose I know that now, that's probably why I'm here.`

`So I was to blame and I should have done something about it when I found out?` asked Carla hesitantly.

`How could you? replied Harry, `and anyway, it wouldn't have stopped. We would have probably carried on no matter what you did.`

`If I'd told your father it might have, it might have even saved the marriage,` replied Carla.

`No it wouldn't have made any difference to us, but I don't know about your marriage`

`How do you know that?` asked Carla curiously.

`Because I just do and if you speak to Sarah, she'll tell you the same.` There was an unfamiliar dimension of certainty in Harry's voice that Carla had not experienced before.

`I still don't understand how it happened,` said Carla.

`It started out quite innocently, through curiosity, the prying inquisitiveness that you have when you are very young. I wanted to know why she was different and she wanted to know why I was different, but for whatever reason, I don't know why, circumstances changed and the sibling relationship began to coalesce into something entirely different.... something we did not understand then or even now.`

`What was different?`

`I think it all changed the first time we kissed... that didn't happen till much later on oddly, but I had never felt that before, a passion, a longing to be needed, to be loved, I don't know. We were growing up and we sensed this empty space, a vacuum between us and we could see it between you and dad, but being together filled this void. I could feel myself slowly dissolving into something, it was like being slowly absorbed into a sponge. Sarah felt the same and whatever it was, we didn't understand it, but when we were together the emptiness wasn't there, it didn't seemed to matter anymore. We blanked out the things we should have thought about I suppose. I don't remember what I was thinking, I just know we were happy when we were together. We desperately needed that and we took it.`

`So it was my fault.` said Carla.

`No that's the point, it wasn't and what could you do? You caught us the once and gave me a right good hiding. But it wasn't going to stop anything.`

`No I didn't think it would,` muttered Carla quietly. She spoke almost as if she had some sort of prior knowledge, or familiarity with the circumstances.

`Maybe you should have told dad, then it might have saved you a lot pain and heartache?`

`I wish to God I had, but I was afraid of what he might do, I didn't want to lose you or Sarah or him and I didn't want anything to change. I just thought it would stop on its own if I ignored it and that would be an end to the matter. `

'But it didn't mum, you knew that.'

'Yes, but the longer I left it the easier it was to push it to the back of my mind and the harder it became to say anything, that's why I ignored you. I just thought that if I didn't think about it then maybe it wasn't really happening.'

'But ignoring us made it worse, you stopped loving us and that just pushed Sarah and me closer together.'

'I know that now, but then well....' Carla began to sob. 'Look at you, what have I done?'

'It's not your fault mum it's really not and I am trying, to sort this thing out, I really am, I just have a problem getting through some of the days at the moment.'

'Like yesterday and this?' said Carla.

'This wasn't supposed to happen.' said Harry unconvincingly, gesturing to his bandaged wrists. Carla started to cry again. 'You'll ruin your makeup,' said Harry smiling.

'I don't want you to die, there's so much I want for you, for you both. You still have the rest of your lives to live. Sarah's is starting again today. You could start a new life if you wanted to.'

'Mum I've had so many things going through my head over the last few years that I'd almost forgotten there was something called life. Some days I do remember, then I'd remember why I try to forget it. I'm sorry, but that's just how I feel, It's like, it's like I'm standing on the edge of cliff looking down knowing I'm just one short breath away from freedom. Just one more breath and I could fly away forever and leave the pain behind. Can you understand that?

'But you said you'd moved on,' implored Carla.

'We both have, but it still comes back. And I can't get rid of this wretched empty feeling deep inside me. Some days I feel really good and then someone says something, something insignificant, unimportant not related to anything in particular and then suddenly there I am, back in this dark place falling endlessly and just waiting to hit the floor and that's when...

`When it happens again will you call me just so we can talk?`

`I'll call you,` replied Harry reassuringly.

`Promise?`

`I promise to call you,` he smiled at Carla to comfort her. `Are you seeing anybody mum?` asked Harry, changing the subject.

`Seeing?` Carla sounded surprised at the question.

`A boyfriend?` clarified Harry

`No. No I can't do that anymore, anyway I like living on my own now.`

`Aren't you lonely?`

`Why do you ask?`

`I just wondered that's all.`

`No. I'm not lonely, not really. I have my memories and the pictures of days in the sun we all spent together... That's enough for me now. That's all I need now.`

`Did you ever love dad?` asked Harry.

`Yes,` replied Carla, a little taken back by the directness of Harry's question. `Yes, I did, I still do actually. Why do you ask?

`Dad doesn't think so.`

`Has he spoken to you?`

`No not directly, it's just something he said some time ago made me wonder, that was all.`

`I did love your dad, I loved him very much, maybe I just didn't show it.` Carla smiled pensively to herself...

`So what happened mum? We never really understood?`

`Life, that's what happens. I made mistakes and one of them changed all our lives and well that just got in the way.` Carla started to gently weep.

`Sorry mum I didn't mean to…`

`That's OK… look I have to go, I don't want to be late,` she hesitated for a moment and gazed at Harry, her mind flashing back to places and times she thought she would never visit again, `I'll pop back in tomorrow to see you, OK?` She quickly brushed away the tears.

`That would be good, I'll look forward to that, now you have a nice day. Everybody wants to see you, they really do, even dad.`

`I'll try.`

`Give Sarah my blessing.`

`I will.` Carla bent over to kiss Harry on the forehead.

`Goodbye mum, I love you.` Carla looked a little surprised.

`I love you too son and don't forget to call me if..`

`Yes mum.` replied Harry reassuringly.

Carla left the room and outside she took a small silver flask from her handbag and took a swig. A doctor passed by and looked at her disapprovingly.

`Medicinal,` she mumbled to herself, then she walked towards the main exit for the last time.

Chapter 12

`It's good to see you dad and you Kathy.` said Nigel greeting them both warmly. `How are you both?` Tony was suddenly filled with a sense of overwhelming pride at the image of his son who had become so consummate and efficient at managing his own life and family social events. The mantle of patriarch had passed so deftly from Tony to Nigel that he hardly noticed how it had bypassed Harry. In some ways, Tony was actually relieved at not being so directly responsible in organising the wedding. Although he still considered himself to be relatively young, he was still only just sixty one, he had suffered a minor heart attack the previous year and not having completely recovered he now found that he became tired much quicker than before and had become strangely despondent. He was also unable to concentrate on anything for long periods. The heart attack had brought about a sudden realisation, or as Nigel used to playfully refer to it "his road to the garden centre moment" regarding his own mortality and had to a large degree, as it probably does with anybody after such an event, changed the way he perceived the priorities of daily life. He now tended to focus on his career as a support mechanism for his life rather than the other way round, but most disturbing of all were his uncharacteristic lapses into short periods of profound emotional distress. These moments occurred in the unlikeliest of circumstances; a kind word or an unexpected compliment even someone simply asking after his wellbeing could suddenly bring tears rushing to his eyes. He would recover quickly, but it marked a distinct change in his sensitivities.

Harry was six years older than Nigel, but had always led a very insular existence, never really attempting to assert himself as the oldest son, (not that there was any obligation to do so) this was a role he was happy to relinquish,. In many families, it was naturally assumed that the eldest child would eventually take on the role of notional guide and mentor to his or her siblings. This was the roll that Nigel had accepted and embraced with great enthusiasm from very early on in his life.

I couldn't recall any particular period which could be clearly and definitively described as Harry's most happiest or felicitous. The closest I could venture would be to say that he gave the impression of someone who was adequately content with life when engaged as a gardener, a profession he had maintained for over five years and from which he derived great satisfaction. After that, he drifted aimlessly between various jobs from which he appeared to take little satisfaction before eventually settling down as a cake and bread maker in a small bakery. I believe he found the late evening and early morning working hours therapeutically conducive, undemanding and strangely calming. The absence of an obligation to socialise with customers, or anybody come to that was an added bonus as far he was concerned. His somnolent declension into the darkened void that would eventually completely envelop him remained virtually undetectable to all but one of us and she couldn't or possibly wouldn't save his soul from the daily torment.

He never married despite having a number of amiable female friends and although they found him to be entertaining and attractive, they each eventually encountered his insensate nature, which undoubtedly precluded them from moving the relationship forward, beyond the primary stages.

Inevitably, there was a sexual aspect to all his relationships, but for reasons I will never fully understand this, paradoxically transpired to be the Achilles heel that condemned any possibility of longevity and sadly each relationship slowly disintegrated almost spiralling out of control like some unseen centrifical force into a whirlwind of effusive desolation. It became painfully obvious that each new relationship left him emotionally worse than the one before and the rapturous paroxysm of euphoric highs from each new liaison were invariably closely followed by a contemptuous   self-loathing vertiginous plunge into the depths of despair. Each new decent a little deeper than the one before.

Nigel gently kissed Kathy on both cheeks and as he did so, she whispered solicitously in his ear.

`This is OK isn't it?` It was impossible for Nigel not to like someone who so obviously cared very deeply about his father and whose heartfelt plea came out of genuine concern for Tony and his children. Grown children seldom respond well to a stepmother who is invariably branded an interloper, a harbinger of the destruction of what was once considered to be a 'happy family' environment and a potential catalyst for unpalatable changes. The question of misappropriation of family assets also sits uneasily with some. Kathy did not generate any of these feelings neither did she emanate any negative traits, in fact she portrayed an image of calm stillness and humility, which had quickly engendered an acquiescent acceptance by the children, but she never took it for granted.

`Yes of course we want you here.` replied Nigel firmly and with a demonstrability which effused Kathy with the comfortable sense of being accepted that she so longed for. He continued, `you have made dad very happy.`

Kathy had only been married to Tony for not quite two years, but she had remained vigilantly circumspect about appearing to replace or relegate their mother to a secondary roll. She had also been married before, but her husband had died unexpectedly from a heart attack nearly twenty years previous when he was only thirty nine and their only child a girl born just nine months before her father's death was severely mentally and physically handicapped and was now permanently confined to an institution. It was partly for this reason that they had never had any further children, which after the unexpected death of her husband was something she had come to sadly regret. An equitable decision made on reasonable and practical grounds at one moment in time, but one which had not unfortunately factored in the possibility of a second disastrous twist of fate at a later date.

The interaction, social intercourse and idiosyncratic nature of family histrionics was something she had only briefly experienced with her own family and now she so desperately needed to be a part of another normal family; a phrase she inherently despised and belligerently avoided using despite the incontrovertible evidence that this was, above all else what she most desired; that she had become blinded to the duplicitous reality of a seriously flawed ideological concept. She so wanted everything in the family to be perfect, the ultimate dream of every mother and wife, but sadly, most dreams are tinged with sadness and naïve flawed optimism is eventually subjugated by a recalcitrant reluctant pragmatism.

Tony was slightly embarrassed by Nigel's declaration, but also inwardly proud as he held out his hand.

Nigel shook his father's hand tightly and Tony smiled.

`It's good to see you to son.`

`It's good to see you dad,` replied Nigel.

`I show Kathy to her seat,` said Tony

`Don't be long, can't keep the bridegroom waiting, don't want to miss our only chance of getting Sarah married off. Mark could still do a runner,` replied Nigel mischievously.

`No chance, I've handcuffed him to the vicar,` replied David sternly without any change of expression. Kathy and Tony smiled at the banter in the way that only two people in a close relationship really can and then continued walking towards the church door.

`They have your sense of humour,` remarked Kathy quietly looking straight ahead as they made their way into the church and smiling to herself.

Tony stopped and looked at Kathy. `You think so?` he said sounding a little surprised.

'Oh yes,' replied Kathy smiling, 'very wicked on the surface, but endearingly passionate and steadfastly loyal underneath.' Tony felt an odd sense of accomplishment at this observation and the sudden realisation of having passed on something good to his children, something which would hopefully last a lifetime.

'Come on, we'd better go in before they start on us,' said Tony cautiously. They made their way to a pew at the front where Kathy sat down next to one of Tony's uncles who they had met a couple of times before. He smiled at them and Tony spoke a few words welcoming him to the occasion then turned around to make his way back to the church entrance. Just as he reached the door, the limousine pulled up with Sarah.

Two bridesmaids, old school friends of Sarah's, dressed in pretty pink coloured dresses with bouquets of white phalaenopsis orchids and ivy leaves stepped carefully out of the car leaving the door open. They started walking a little coquettishly towards the church to the admiring glances of Nigel and David, but Sarah stayed in the car and beckoned Tony to come over to the car.

'Dad?...' Questioned Sarah, just one word, but saying so many things.

'You look absolutely beautiful darling,' interrupted Tony in a subtle attempt to divert the course of a conversation, which he thought for some inexplicable reason, he might not want to have at that moment.

'Thank you dad,' replied Sarah, who took the complement in a not unsurprisingly unexpected matter of fact way. Her expression and demeanour indicated a sense of apprehension, which Tony had sensed immediately.

'Could you get in for a moment?'

'Of course darling,' he slipped in beside her.

'Not having a change of heart?' asked Tony with some trepidation.

`I don't' know, it's just that... well I can't help wondering if... am I doing the right thing?`

`Of course you are,` assured Tony. `Mark's a good man and he loves you. You deserve this, you both deserve this.`

`But I haven't told him everything dad and I feel that, well he should know the truth and I feel as if I'm being unfaithful before we are even married and I don't know whether I should tell him now, before or.. `

`Now stop right there.` uttered Tony, with a harsh almost admonitory tone, gently ladened with paternalism. He thought for a few seconds before continuing. `Whatever has happened before belongs in the past and that's where you must leave it.`

`But the past is what makes me the person I am,` replied Sarah.

`Only a small part of it. All that you are is what you are today and all that you want is in the future. The past should be left where it is. It's finished business, its dead, it has gone and you have to forget about it if you want a future.`

`It's just that...` Sarah paused, `sometimes I feel the past controls me, it like a shadowy hand that comes out of the darkness and tries to pull me back, to take over.. `

`The past is the time for experience and learning and making mistakes, many mistakes and we all make many mistakes,` replied Tony. He paused for a few moments to think about those words, `but one day you must leave all that behind. I know you can never completely forget these things, so that is why you must place them somewhere out of harm's way - into a little memory box and when you have done that you close the lid and you keep it closed. All the good things that have happened to you, you put into another box and you leave that box open so you can see them every day. If you do this, you will be safe. The future is the time for hopes and dreams, that's what you have to hold onto. You must not let the past dictate what happens in the future, if you do there will never be a future and your past will eventually consume you.`

`Don't you think it could change everything if Mark found out afterwards?`

`Found out what?` asked Tony.

`The truth,` replied Sarah.

`You mean his perception of the truth, there is a vast difference you know.`

`I don't understand dad,` said Sarah.

Tony pulled the car door closed and asked the driver if he could have five minutes alone with his daughter. Tony waited until the driver had left the car and shut his door.

`If you disclose to Mark what happened to you in the cold light of day, to unburden the unjustifiable guilt you feel then and in all due respects to Mark; and I apologise if I do him a disservice with my disingenuous rant, but he would probably come to one inexorable conclusion and the pure dynamics of that one action could change forever the parameters of your existing relationship can you see that?`

`What conclusion?` enquired Sarah anxiously.

`That you were a willing participant?` replied Tony a little bluntly.

`But I wasn't, he raped me,` replied Sarah almost shouting and starting to cry. Tony put his hands up to gently cup Sarah's face and calm her down.

`I know that, you know that, but would Mark?`

`I don't know.` A single tear began to run down Sarah's face and she wiped it away with the back of her hand.

`But your relationship would change forever wouldn't it?

`Yes I suppose so,` replied Sarah reluctantly.

`You do agree?` Tony repeated the question to prompt a definitive answer, but Sarah was unsure why.

`Yes, yes it would,` she eventually muttered.

135

`But if for instance one day you had a baby and on that day you told Mark about the things that happened to you so many years ago and how you thought you would never be really happy again. And on this day you told him you were happier than you had ever been and that it was Mark who had made you happy, then do you not think that he might look on what had happened to you in a different light?`

`I don't know,` replied Sarah hesitantly.

`Alright let me put it another way,` continued Tony, `do you think he would look at the past events with more or less compassion and concern on that particular day?`

`More probably,` replied Sarah.

`So his perception of truth, the way it effects you both and the interpretation of an event is, to a large degree, governed by a change in the specific moment of disclosure?` continued Tony.

`Yes I suppose so.`

`So time and the perception of truth can change?`

`Yes.` replied Sarah cautiously, still a little unsure where this was all leading.

`So it would not be wrong to wait for a better time?

`No.`

`Good.`

`Do you realise that people die in wars not just because they are shot or blown up, but because it's the just wrong day for them.`

`Wrong day,` queried Sarah, `I don't understand.`

`If they were in the same place five years later or maybe five years earlier they would probably be on holiday instead of fighting and they would have missed it and they wouldn't have died after all. You see its destiny which places them where they are and truth which decides why they are there and how they are connected, which is why picking the right time can change the outcome and your destiny do you see?`

`I'm not sure about that,` replied Sarah, sounding a little confused, 'it still feels like a deceit.'

`It's only deception if the intention is to deceive for personal gain, but that isn't the case. You both stand to lose if you tell him now and all because of something over which you had no control.

`You think so?' said Sarah

`It's what politicians do - they bury bad news in a torrent of good news, that way it becomes swamped and lost forever. Do you see?`

`Yes I see what you mean,` replied Sarah

`Try it, what have you got to lose?` implored Tony, 'only what you are about to lose.'

`So nothing I suppose,' Sarah paused to consider what had been said, 'but what if he finds out before I pick the time?`

`He won't, how can he?` there's only your mother, me, David and Nigel who know and we will never say anything.`

`And Harry,` added Sarah looking at Tony despondently. She could see the reasoning, but Harry was the weak link.

`Harry will never say anything,` replied Tony.

`So I don't tell him?`

`Not today, one day when the time is right, you will know when, but not today. Even Mark will have things from the past that he keeps tucked away in his memory box.`

`You think so?`

`Yes I do, we all have. Look I want to read you something. I wrote it for my speech, but maybe it would be better if I read it to you now and then you decide what you must do.` He took a creased letter from inside his pocket, unfolded it and flattened it out on his leg.

137

My dearest darling daughter this is your day.

And on this day, you will feel happy and maybe just a little sad.

And tears may even come.

And when they do, don't hold back let them fall.

For they will wash the past away.

And after the tears, only the memories of happy days will remain.

You have given your heart and soul to this man and he to you.

He will protect you and guide you through your life together.

But I will always be there for you.

I will not let you down and we will always be together.

Be strong and enjoy the moment.

For this day will soon be over and will never come again.

Tomorrow is the beginning of the rest of your life.

So always remember I love you my dearest darling daughter.

And I will always be thinking of you.

Sarah kissed her father and they both smiled and then they opened the doors stepped out and walked arm in arm to the church.

Chapter 13

Carla stood outside the main door of the hospital languorously holding a cigarette, watching the grey smoke spiral slowly upwards swirling to the heavens, before being swept away by the warm summer breeze.

Her thoughts were on Sarah's wedding later that morning, but her mind was being distracted by what Harry had said. Something was troubling her, something else she was unsure of, amongst all the things of which she was uncertain and she quietly prayed to God that one day she would understand everything that had happened in her life and why it had unfolded the way it had.

The gentle felicity of the autumn sun tempered the turmoil in her tortured soul and warmed a body that had sadly grown old and fragile over the last few years. Desolation had subtlety sequestrated her very being and now dominated a mind now constantly assailed by Manichaean conflict between light and darkness. Her troubled senses only assuaged by the regular intake of alcohol.

Since she had been living alone, she had lost the desire to eat properly, now existing solely on an eclectic diet of tinned tuna - which she ate directly from the tin, extricating each chunk with a teaspoon - or cold baked beans, which she ate with white bread and a Tesco's own brand scotch whiskey. This, the established fare of box dwellers, tramps, students off campus and those on the final journey to oblivion.

She had also acquired a taste for Jack Daniels and blackcurrant juice (a ghastly concoction) when she could afford it, but that wasn't often. The desultory nature of her diminished lifestyle had wreaked havoc on her limbs in a relatively short time and they were now bony and angular. Her beautiful skin once burnished like gold by the Mediterranean sun was now wan and translucent and hung from her bones like folds of thin leather.

For a few seconds Carla shut her eyes, the noise of the traffic faded away and she was transported to another place where she could forget the life that had gone so terribly wrong and just be someone different for a while. Many years ago on a holiday in Tuscany, Tony and the children had gone to a lake every day and she had stayed behind because she didn't like swimming. She would just lay in the sun at the villa listening to the sound of silence, apart that is from the odd cicada and sparrow and she thought that was as near to heaven as she would ever be. So why couldn't she have a normal life again, like everybody else she thought, but of course nobody else had a normal life it just appeared that way. Beneath the façade there were always the secrets and lies mostly hidden from sight, but still there just below the surface slowly eating away at the fabric that surrounded a relationship till one day it would stand shamefully naked and exposed for all to see. These were the nebulous illusions created to obfuscate the truth and confuse reality and all this would be gone forever in another existence.

The traffic sound suddenly returned with its stark and sonorously clattering ensemble and with this resumption of reality she reluctantly opened her eyes. She took another small swig of whiskey from the silver flask, put it back in her handbag, dropped her cigarette in a butt bin and walked over to a taxi parked in the rank and through the open passenger window spoke to the cab driver, `Can you take me to St Peters Church in Camden town?`

The cabby replied jovially (in a stereo-typical cockney accent but with a distinctive trace of Wales) `No problem love jump in.`

`Thank you,` said Carla resting back in her seat. For some odd reason the cabby's accent suddenly conjured up a vision of Dick Van-Dyke in Mary Poppins, which was even more bizarre because she also remembered that he had the worst cockney accent she had ever heard in a film.

`Getting married are we love?` asked the cabby with casual indifference to the odd connotation of his question.

`Married!` replied Carla, surprised at his assumption.

`The hat thing, the way you're dressed it's very nice, it looks like you're off to get married.`

`Oh I see,` replied Carla who had totally forgotten she was wearing a large fascinator.'

`Oh no, not me, my daughter. I've given up men. Twice married, twice, divorced that's enough for me in one lifetime. I don't understand them anymore. I don't want anything more to do with them.` She thought that declaration would guarantee a relatively quiet journey to the church. She didn't feel much like engaging in taxi chat and the whiskey was beginning to have that beautifully dulling affect she craved, but she was wrong for she had not taken into account the robust, resilient and loquacious nature of the London taxi driver.

`Ah! my wife says that about me every day. Sad thing is I'm actually beginning to agree with her. I mean if you're really think about it, we're a pretty useless bunch of idiots, just look at all the problems in the world? And who causes them all? Men that's who. If I had my way, I'd have the whole lot put down at birth. Old Pontius had the right idea. Country's never been the same since they stabbed Maggie in the back the bastards, 'scuse me French, now we're paying for it. She had it all sorted out, she knew how to handle men. Bloody Argies didn't know what hit 'em. Mind you, they should have known better. They had one of their own once and she was a clever girl, so they had no excuse forgetting about the implacable attitude of you women. Took a big gang of miserable double crossing bastards to sneak up behind her and stab her in the back. Bit like poor old Caesar stabbed him in the back too. So I know how you feel love.`

`I think you're being a little hard on yourself,` replied Carla, `nobody's perfect.` She was a little taken back by his refreshing outburst of self-deprecating invective. It actually made her smile.

`You don't see women starting wars, do you?` asked the cabby vehemently.

`No except for Bou..,` said Carla, attempting to reply, but the cabby interrupted politely before she could reply…

`No course not… nor do they go round sticking up the price of diesel. I mean have you seen the price lately, they're having a laugh aren't they? Poor old cabbies trying to earn a honest bleeding crust, 'scuse me French and all the bleeding Arabs just sitting on their on their bloody arses, 'scuse me French, in their golden palaces and yanking our bleeding chains,.. they're all blokes.`

`The Arabs do have all the oil..,` suggested Carla cautiously, taking timely advantage of the cabby having to take a short breath and concentrate while strategically negotiating his cab into the correct lane between two enormous lorries which appeared to portend one of those horrendous concertina sandwich accidents that she had read about in the Daily Mail. Of one particular incident she recalled reading about, the two lorries had come together and squashed a car into half its normal width. Fortunately on this occasion the lorry to the left of the cab decided to turn left and her concerns were allayed. She breathed a small sigh of relief. The cabby seemed to be completely unaware of their fleeting brush with mortality, but then maybe this was a normal everyday occurrence for a taxi driver, she mused to herself.

`.. and that's all they have, continued Carla. `so I suppose they have to sell it for the best price they can get.` She quietly congratulated herself on what she considered to be an astute and succinct if slightly precocious analysis of the disposition of world supplies of oil and the commercial acumen of the Arabs before the cabby could reply she continued… `Nobody wants to buy their sand?` Feeling herself irresistibly drawn into the conversation not so much as to exchange the pleasantries on the condemnation of the male of the species, but strangely to actually defend them. The cabby had initiated the conversation from an unexpected perspective and this had caught her imagination as well as slightly off balance. Somehow he had managed to place her in a diametrically opposed position to one she would

142

normally have adopted, but she felt good about that. It felt refreshingly liberating to be intellectually stimulated even at this pedestrian level. She seldom had conversations these days that progressed anywhere beyond supermarket chatter. That was something she sadly missed from being married.

`Well I suppose you have a point there,` muttered the driver reluctantly. `Alright then look at another bloke, Jesus?` mused the cabby now slightly deflated, but with a sense of expectation and anticipation as he switched the conversation to the dangerous subject of religion. Historically a strictly taboo topic in a taxi, if you wanted a decent tip. It was all too easy to unintentionally offend.

`Jesus!` repeated Carla a little surprised at the tenuous introduction of an iconic deity. He had managed to catch her off guard with that pronouncement and had simultaneously diverted the conversation deftly down another side road she hadn't expected. Carla was now having a problem following his unpredictable train of thought.

`Yea Jesus, Jesus Christ our saviour.` He crossed himself with a hasty genuflection. `I mean who was it who nailed him to a bloody cross? Well it wasn't the bloody women's institute was it, no it was men again what done that. Nothing better to do at Easter you see. Didn't fancy the chocolate, no football on the tele so they get hammered on a few bottles of the local vino collapso then pop down the market for a bit of gratuitous violence and mindless victimisation of a minor religious figure and before you know it they've gone and crucified the poor sod. Bloody tossers, sorry love, but injustice and racial intolerance just gets right up my nose...`

`I thought that...` said Carla inquisitively before the cabby interjected yet again. She was going to have to be more forthright if she was ever going to insert herself with any credibility into this conversation. His was a naturally garrulous occupation and he was proving to be a proficient personage and eloquent exponent of his calling.

`I know what you're going to say,` said the cabby, but not in an arrogant way, `he was crucified by the Jews and him being a Jew it was their call. The Romans done the deed, but the Jews was the instigators bit like Millwall playing away at Portsmouth. Poor old Pontius pilot didn't know what to do. He would have been perfectly happy just sitting down with a few of bottles of wine and having a few mates round for a quiet Friday night in, watching the quarter finals and having some intellectual chit chat, but no, up pops a few drunken right wing radicals, who obviously don't watch football and they want this trouble maker out of the frame; so what can Pontius do? Nothing! He has to keep them happy so that was it, job done. It would have been all different if Jesus had been a woman. None of your religious wars, because women would have sat down had a nice G and T, talked about handbags and shoes and any geographical or religious issues would have been amicably sorted out without any fuss. Don't remember too many ladies being crucified do you?`

`No but...` replied Carla, who thought this was a bit sexist and demeaning and was going to say so, but the cabby cut in again before she could continue..

`You see deep down we've always been a little bit afraid of them, because we always knew they were more clever than us, but the real problem is, we just don't really understand how they work, we just think we do and they know that and deep down we know they know we know that.` he paused for a few seconds to think about what he had just said and to let his brain catch up before continuing... `if you get my meaning`

`I do but...` replied Carla with a hint of a smile at this revelation, but having been thwarted twice before in her attempts to intercede, she decided now was not the best time to interrupt, not while he was in full flow anyway.

`...if only we would listen just a little bit more to what they, sorry I mean you have to say - and I mean really listen, not just stand around in La-la land playing pockets billiards, jingling the loose change in our pockets and waiting for our turn to start banging on about any old load of cobblers, then I think we might begin to understand them, sorry again, I

144

meant you... then I think we might be getting somewhere, but the chances of that happening...` he suddenly stopped, realising that Carla had finished her last reply with a "But" which probably meant she was going to say something else... `sorry love did you say something?`

`Eh no, no it doesn't matter now,` replied Carla quietly, still smiling gently inside at the irony of the statement he had just made, which had obviously completely passed him by.

`I have to work evenings most days to make a decent wage and let me tell you it's a bloody battlefield out there after the clubs kick out on Friday night. Blokes kicking seven bails of shit out of each other all over nothing at all, mind you some of the young girls are getting in on the act now, but I think that's your lot just fighting back after years of injustice, inequality and oppression. I mean women don't really get a chance to express themselves do they? There ain't one half decent painter or composer did you know that? A few politicians, but mostly they get shot or blown up. Mind you a lot of men get shot as well, but that's all down to the bevy again.`

`There are quite a few doctors who...` started Carla, but the driver immediately cut in again.

`You're right, there are a few, but all your fancy Harley street quacks are blokes and if somebody does some really amazing surgical thing like an head transplant, then I bet it's a bloke who gets all the glory. I mean look at darning, that's a dying art, my Blodwyn used to darn my socks but not anymore, bloody well refuses point blank. Says it's cheaper to buy a new pair than darn a hole, but that's just waste and we are trying to save the planet so I thought that was a contribution, but she wouldn't have none of it. Now that's something that women invented, then men nicked the idea so they could stitch up the bleeding great holes they blow in each other. If I was a woman then I'd have a go at something artistic to help your lot out. Mind you I don't fancy the baby bit unless they'd sorted out the mechanics. Never liked the sound of it much, I mean it all sounds a bit painful trying to pass a bleeding great watermelon from what I can make out, if you know what I mean. I have enough trouble with...` but he stopped talking suddenly realising where the conversation was going.

`So you might consider having a baby if...` said Carla tongue in cheek, leaving the sentence precariously balanced in mid-air...

`No not really love, just hypothesising. The point I was trying to make was you can't get a big head in a little hat can you? If you know what I mean. Your gonner split the 'at if you're not careful, more darning and that never sounded like a lot of fun to me. So another technical cock up for man if you excuse the pun. Reminded me of when my Blodwyn was having ours. Have you got any kids? Course you have you're just going to your daughter's wedding aren't you. Silly arse, me that is, not you love, see what I mean brain like a Muppet, I really don't know how we've existed this long. It's a bloody miracle if you ask me.`

`How many do you have?` asked Carla.

`Just the two, boys God help us. Two more men in the world to bugger things up, well maybe not if I can help it.`

`I'm sure they won't be that bad,` replied Carla reminiscing.

`No you're probably right, a bit unfair on them really, doing them a grave disservice. They're as good as gold. They were little angels when they was growing up. I used to love being home during the day just to be with 'em. Used to work nights just so I could be there and watch them learning how to do everything. I was there when both of them took their first steps, unbelievable, never thought that those little bundles crawling around the floor would suddenly stand up on their own feet one day, didn't see possible, but they did. Never ceases to amaze me. Christ it used to break my bleeding heart some days. I used to look at them and hope to God they'd have a good life, they were only small, but you still know what life's got piled up waiting for 'em, well some of it, not all of it obviously. Used to make me feel so proud just watching them, I could never get over that. How perfect they were, hair, teeth, I used to run me big monkey mitts, over their perfect skin, thought it was absolutely bloody marvellous. I was fascinated by their little fingers and toes, I used to love playing with their toes, so small so perfect. It's a blooming miracle. Wouldn't have missed those years for the world. It's a bloody shame they have to grow up. Broke my bleeding heart the first day they went to school, think I cried more than they did. Right bloody state I was in... Carla thought she could see a small tear in his eye looking up at his rear view mirror.

'So how many kids do you have?` he asked.

'Five, no well four actually one died very young,` replied Carla quietly.

'I'm sorry, I didn't mean to..,` he stopped talking for a moment, not knowing for sure where he should go. For once, he was lost for words.

'No it's OK I've come to terms with it now,` replied Carla suddenly aware of his unease.

'That must have been heart-rending, I can't imagine what you must of felt like inside?` said the cabby quietly empathising with Carla.

'It was a long time ago, but she was my first so it made me feel suspicious and mistrustful.` Life was suddenly precarious and uncertain and I hadn't experienced that before.

'Suspicious off whom?` asked the cabby sounding slightly curious, but suddenly becoming aware of the deeper implications of what and how his innocent question could irretrievably move the conversation precariously close to a metaphysical dimension which would overstep the normally benign cabby-passenger relationship whatever that might be, but it was too late, the words had slipped past his lips.

'God that's who,` replied Carla with an impassioned honesty that spoke volumes about sadness and remorse; and in one breath carelessly damned the iniquities of religious sycophants. 'It made me suspicious that he could do that. I began to speculate as to why this paradoxical figure, someone who trafficked in hurt and love with equanimity and automaticity without question or accountability or consideration for the consequences would do that. But I came to terms with it eventually, I suppose we all look for someone to blame and he was easy, but I was wrong...` said Carla almost repentantly, `I know that now.`

`That must have made things really hard for the other children?` asked the cabby almost retrospectively.

`Hard. why?` replied Carla with slight hesitation. Any preconceptions she may have held about cabbies now firmly put aside.

`Well you give all your love to the first child don't you? I know I did. I love my two boys both the same but Eric, the first one was special. That's the miracle child isn't it? I mean until you have the first one you don't really know if everything works do you. I remember looking at him the moment he was born and thinking my God he's a real person and one day he will grow up and be able to speak to me; and the missus and me made him. I was blubbering all over the shop I was so happy, but in the same instant I was suddenly aware of my own mortality. I realised that as he had been born so one day I would die, it's one of those defining moments, the reality of impermanence. I remember the nurses had to sit me down and give me a cup of tea. I was in such a state. ......you'd have thought it was me that 'ad just dropped the sprog, not the old lady.` He stopped talking for a moment as he negotiated a large busy roundabout.

`As it is he's a bloody Chelsea supporter so even 'e wasn't perfect,` he muttered mournfully.

`I never got over losing her,` muttered Carla.

`I don't think anybody could get over that love,` replied the cabby with heartfelt sympathy.

`You're right about what you said.` said Carla.

`About what?` said the cabby, a little unsure about which one of his sweeping philosophical ramblings she was alluding to.

`About loving the first child, I could never love the others quite the same. I was always afraid of getting to close to them, just in case, you know?` Carla spoke the words with an almost tactile edge of regret. `I stood back, I was.... I was like a bystander, I became a reluctant spectator to my own life. I felt safer not being involved, I couldn't be hurt anymore if I.....` but that was so selfish of me, I can see that now but...`

`Terrible price to pay that, but I know what you mean,` replied the driver, `It's like the first day they walk to school on their own. They say goodbye then off they trot up the road and you want to run after them and hold their hand and protect them, . . but you don't. You just hope you've taught them everything they need to know about roads and people and life, but in the back of your mind, you know it happens every day somewhere to someone. You don't stop loving them, but with each passing day you start to prepare a small part of yourself for the unpleasant things that might happen and to do this you have to prepare a shield, this invisible barrier, against the reality of life and you just hope you never have to use it. Every day they comeback unharmed, but still it's there tucked away deep in a dark little corner of your brain. One single cell, with one single thought in it and just occasionally quite unexpectedly you have this blinding flash of . . . well you know...` He spoke with a sense of understanding, compassion and synergy which she was beginning to realise was utterly wasted on driving a taxi, or maybe it wasn't.

`I've been afraid all my life,` declared Carla passionately, `that's why I stopped loving mine, it was the only way I could protect myself from what might happen to them.`

`But nothing ever did, did it?` asked the cabby, almost answering his own question.

'No nothing did, they're all fine I even have a granddaughter now, but I never learned to love them again, I just forgot how to. And now it's too late.'

'Too late!' the cabby exclaimed, 'It's never too late to love someone, especially your children, you should give it another try love.'

'It's not about trying it's more about being able to. I've built my own protective wall between us, but it's so high; I still love them, but I'm so afraid to show it in case something happens that I still stand a long way back behind the wall and because I'm so far back I can't sense how they feel anymore,' replied Carla, 'can you understand that?'

'Yes I can,' said the cabby, 'but you're missing out on so much just on the off chance of something going wrong, but it probably never will.'

Carla said nothing for a few moments, deliberating carefully over what the cabby had said.

'I suppose you're right,' she replied with a resigned acceptance.

'You've got to try to love the people that matter to you and hope they love you back, if they don't then what have you lost?'

'Not much, well nothing really,' replied Carla.

'Exactly and at least you tried, so it's a no brainer.'

'I suppose so when you put it like that,' said Carla fully appreciating the pedestrian wisdom of his words.

'Here we are then St Peters, just in time by the looks of things,' said the driver.

'Thank you and thanks for.. '

'Don't mention it,' said the cabby, 'all in a day's work sorting out the problems of the world that's what we do really.' He pulled up outside the church and Carla stepped out. She turned to pay the driver, who glanced quickly at the meter then turned back to Carla. It was only then that she took notice of who he was. This kindly face, not someone she knew or someone she was ever likely to meet again, but someone to whom she had over the last twenty minutes with unbridled ease and innocent abandonment opened up her heart and her secret world and shared her deepest thoughts and regrets over what had happened in her past, all her hopes and fears for what might happen in the future and the angst and lonely hopelessness she was experiencing right now and all for the price of a cab fare.

`That's £8.90 love,` said the cabby. Carla handed him a ten pound note. She had probably confessed more of herself to this man in the time it took to complete this one short journey than she had to any other living soul during the whole of her life up to that moment. For the price of a decent bottle of wine she had been shown a way to exorcise the emptiness that bibulously filled her body and afforded her the luxury of a valediction to her past. This had been the catharsis for the wrath and the fury that had burnt away her heart. But from that moment she felt the profound sadness that had overwhelmed her for so long begin to abate, but for how long would the brief reprieve last she thought, how long before the demons returned.

`Keep the change,` said Carla as the driver offered the coins.

`Thank you and remember what I said.` He held up his index finger as if he were a school teacher making a point and he smiled.

`I will,` she said `and thank you.` He drove off and Carla turned back to look at the church but didn't move for a moment. She seemed a little uneasy at first, unsure of her surroundings and took a few moments to get her bearings before making her way slowly towards the church. Her mind flashed back to what had been said in the taxi and she made a promise not to forget what she had agreed to do.

Chapter 14

`Hello Mum are you OK?` said Nigel. Carla kissed him on the cheek, hugged him tightly and whispered `I love you son.` There was a sense of quiet desperation in the embrace, as if her very existence depended on his response.

`I love you too mum how have you been?` asked Nigel, a little surprised at her uncharacteristically animated display of affection.

`I haven't been too well for a while, but I think I'm OK now. I've missed you, I've missed all of you.`

`Well you should come over and see us more often.` replied Nigel, `You're always welcome you know that. Katie misses seeing you.`

`Thank you yes I will. I would like that very much, I'd love to see more of Katie - now she's growing up.` she paused for a second thinking of Katie and her mind inexplicably flashed back nearly thirty five years to when Sarah was four years old. She could clearly visualise her happily playing with Harry in the garden, it seemed like only yesterday, the details were so clear. She continued to watch them smiling and running around the sand pit enjoying the brief moment before she felt a tear uncontrollably well up from nowhere and cruelly the moment was snatched away as she became suddenly paralyzed by this illusion of innocent gentility which she now knew so cleverly masked the carnage of reality which would eventually envelope and destroy so much.

`I had a couple of drinks in the taxi so I am a bit squiffy, is that alright?`

`Off course it is, it's a wedding that's what we do, get pissed. I've had a couple as well, everybody probably has so I don't think anybody will notice.`

'I needed some Dutch courage... to face your father and Kathy,' she explained apologetically.

'I understand,' said Nigel nodding and smiling sympathetically.

Carla took a couple of steps backwoods to look at him. 'You've lost a little weight.'

'So everybody keeps telling me. It's very busy at the factory at the moment - I suppose it's all the stress that does it,' replied Nigel, a little surprised that Carla had noticed. It had been some time since they last met.

'It suits you,' she replied.

'You've lost weight to,' said Nigel.

'I don't eat quite so much these days,' replied Carla. In fact she ate far less these days. Since the divorce, which was, nearly six years ago she had lost her appetite and most days she would eat a thin slice of toast for breakfast without any accompaniment, except for the occasional first drink of the day. For lunch, she might open a tin of tuna, which she would invariably eat from the tin not even bothering to put in on a plate. She could see no point in making a dish dirty just to wash it up a few minutes later. Dinner was a similar ritual, a poignant wretched process conducted painfully slowly in the vanishing daylight of a fading life, but this time accompanied by the last drink of the day before retiring early to bed.. Watching soap operas on the television about other people living their lives held no interest for her anymore. Nothing seemed to be as real. In the final minutes just before sunset the sounds of the world would be slowly extinguished by the deathly stillness of darkness sweeping over the village like an astral magicians sweeping cloak. No more the distant vibration of other people's lives, scurrying and scuttling in a vertiginous helter skeltar, endeavouring to complete their daily errands and tasks before the day was gone.

Are they contemptuous of her timidity she wondered, for she made no contribution to the reticent gentility of this reassuring communal hustle, this bustle of social activity that enraptured everyone but excluded her. She was incarcerated in her personal living mausoleum a refuge of solitude, despair and remorse.

The recalcitrant banality of their existence would confront her daily, but there was no antipathy for they didn't know she was there and they didn't know how she felt. This desultory and soulless self-loathing existence had finally taken over and had almost completely exsanguinated the last remnants of spirit from her soul. For hours she would sit in the darkness, for the light would only remind her of where she was and not where she wanted to be. She could dream in the dark and fantasise about how things could have been if.... Yes she did feel bitter, she had done no wrong, but events that she couldn't control, had simply overwhelmed her.

David who had been standing by the entrance to the church with his back to the road turned and noticed Carla and Nigel talking and made his way over smiling reassuringly at Carla as he approached.

`Hello mum,` he said affectionately, `You look beautiful.` She pulled him toward her, almost nervously at first for reasons she couldn't explain and as she held him close, she held out her hand in a gesture to Nigel to join them in this embrace. While she held them, her thoughts went to Harry in the hospital and Sarah about to be married and all that had passed. The warmth of the embrace lifted her spirits and instilled a fragile confidence, for the years of living alone listening to silence had made her cautious and wary of forging relationships, but she felt at ease with her sons and could feel a shallow sense of self-belief returning.

The years she had spent alone had withered her natural spontaneity, a disagreeable trait in her mind, for she had always enjoyed and derived great satisfaction from the heartfelt approbation of a receptive audience, to a moment of easy candour and levity. She had become apprehensive and guarded about emotional commitment and found herself increasingly reluctant to employ affection for fear of embarrassment or rejection.

In her bedroom at night and fearful of the darkness and the tiny indiscriminate unexplainable creaks that peppered the hours before dawn, she had taken to lodging a chair behind the bedroom door and kept a baseball bat under the bed. The house was far less secure than it used to be as the comprehensive intruder alarm system that had been installed some years ago, complete with external security lights and electric gates to the driveway no longer operated properly. The gates had even taken to opening on their own from time to time. Another example of inanimate obstinacy, which seemed to plague her waking hours.

Fortunately, some years previously, Carla had meticulously planted pyracantha bushes around the entire walled perimeter of the house and these now stood six foot high and with their extremely painful thorns were a remarkably efficient and inexpensive defence against any intruder who might consider circumventing the main gates (if they were shut that is) and gain entry over the walls. Carla reasoned that anybody negotiating the wall and landing on the bush would almost immediately jump back over the wall once they had experienced the excruciating pain inflicted by thorns, but despite all these precautions, she still felt vulnerable. Just being alone allowed her imagination to cavort riotously and uncontrollably with her senses and her protective enclave now felt more like a prison. She was going to move to somewhere much smaller, but the thought of leaving the place where she had once been happy always stopped her making the final decision. This was tempered with all that had happened with Harry and Sarah

'Where's Sarah?' Carla enquired.

'She'll be here in a minute,' replied David. 'Mark is already inside.'

'Mark!' enquired Carla a little puzzled as she didn't recognise the name.

'That is who's she marrying,' confirmed David a little concerned that Carla didn't seem to know his name.

`That's right. His name was on the invitation wasn't it?` replied Carla `I've become a little absent minded these days.`

`Do you want to go in?` David enquired.

`I supposed I'd better. Don't want to wander in pissed half way through do I and make a spectacle of myself?` She smiled reassuringly at David, `Only joking darling, is your father here yet?`

`He's already inside,` confirmed David.

`Is.. she' here?` asked Carla dryly.

`You're not going to make a scene are you mum? asked David a little surprised at the tone in her voice. All the disagreeable machinations of a divorce had long since been settled and Carla had known about Kathy for over two years.

`No I just wondered that's all. Anyway it's all quite civilised now, we even talk,` replied Carla politely. She smiled to herself.

`I show you to your seat,` said David, Carla looked at him and smiled disarmingly.

`That would be lovely. Thank you.` David took her arm and walked her slowly and proudly into the church.

`Sarah's very happy now mum,` said David quietly as they walked to the pew.

`Is she?` questioned Carla with a hint of uncertainty.

`Yes,` confirmed David.

`Does she blame me?` asked Carla tentatively.

`For what,` enquired David, uncertain as to what she was alluding to and wary of making a spurious assumption. His training as a contract lawyer had fostered an acute level of circumspection when drawn into any discussions where the subject matter was potentially contentious.

`For what happened,` replied Carla `.. when she was young.`

David was a little surprised at Carla's unexpected reference to a period in their lives that had been almost forgotten about and of which they had not spoken of for many years.

`She doesn't blame you for anything, only ever wanted you to love her, that's all. She could deal with everything else, but she needed your love.`

`Well I'm here so maybe this is the time to put things straight once and for all. I do love her you know, I love you all very much.` Although this was an impassioned declaration from Carla, deep down she obviously still had some reservations.

`Then tell her mum, that's all she needs. Just to know that, will mean so much to her especially today,` replied David.

`I will, I really will, I'll speak to her,… today.`

`Have you been to see Harry?` asked David.

`I saw him this morning, he seems OK, but he won't be coming, they're keeping him in for a few more days,` replied Carla.

`Maybe that's best,` added David thoughtfully.

`It would have been nice if he could have been here,` said Carla. `It would have made the day….a turning point for everything.`

`Maybe,` replied David thoughtfully. He smiled and turned back to walk towards the main door, but Carla spoke again…

`I really did try you know I just didn't know what to do,` David turned back to Carla.

`It doesn't matter now. We've all moved on,` replied David. `It's over it's done.`

`Do you really think so?` asked Carla.

`Yes, yes I do.` replied David confidently. Carla looked at him, but said nothing and sat down at the end of the pew.

David turned back and walked towards the rear exit. Carla looked around the congregation and made eye contact with Kathy, who was at the other end of the row. They

157

smiled reservedly at each other. A few more guests arrived and David and Nigel took their places at the front of the Church just behind Carla. The organ began to play the wedding march, the congregation rose to their feet and Tony entered the church with Sarah on his arm. As they arrived at the alter the vicar gestured for them to sit down. Sarah turned to Carla and smiled.

`Firstly I would like to welcome everybody here today for the wedding of Sarah and Mark. I have known Sarah for many years so this is a particularly special day for me too. . . Just before we start I would like to say that I have noticed that there are a few babies here, today and to the parents I would say, that if they happen to cry out during the ceremony then they should not be concerned. They are just asking to be comforted probably because they sense they are in an unusual environment. The sound of a child crying out only enhances what really happens here today, because I believe that when a child cries out, she or he is simply seeking confirmation that there is someone there, someone who loves them and wants to protect them and will always be there and they need this constant reassurance. Maybe we all need this reassurance to one degree or another, even when we are no longer children, but we just get out of the habit of crying out and we forget how to ask. Jesus Christ is a little like that parent, always there, always ready to listen and comfort...`

Carla was suddenly overwhelmed by the profoundly poignant and seemingly personal dimension of the words even though she knew it they were not directed specifically at her. She could remember Sarah crying many times in the morning when she was a child, but she had been unable to comfort her.

The vicar continued...

`...so if we have to wait a few minutes here and there then so be it.` he looked at Sarah and Mark and started the service..

`We are gathered here today to celebrate the marriage of Sarah and Mark and …`

Chapter 15

After the service everybody walked the few yards to the reception in a marquee at the rear of the Lonely Shepherd pub just a few minutes away. It was a lovely day for a party and the ensemble, walking casually up the street, all chatting animatedly made a charming contribution to a beautiful summer's day in the village. After Sarah and Mark had welcomed everybody at the entrance they all sat down and continued their conversations while awaiting the waitresses who were beginning to bring out the champagne. Sarah rose from the table and walked over to Tony.

`Thanks for the chat in the car dad it helped a lot.`

`Just need to sort Harry out now,` replied Tony philosophically, but sounding a little sad.

`Should I go and see him?` asked Sarah.

`I don't know if that will help,' replied Tony, ` but I don't suppose it can do any harm.` He looked strangely sallow and withdrawn.

For no particular reason Sarah's attention was suddenly drawn to the drained expression that was palpably visible in her father's face, she thought about how everything that had happened had undoubtedly affected him one way or another and wondered if it had changed him from the way he might have been had everything turned out a little differently. Had anyone else really noticed? she wondered. No family on earth ever really existed in a trouble free utopian paradise she knew that much, they just survived in a morality vacuum each one only slightly different from the rest depending on how much morality leaked in. He was neither Harry's or her biological father, but he was still deeply affected by how life had treated them both.

`I'll go tomorrow maybe, before we leave for France,` said Sarah.

`Only if you want to,` replied Tony, `you may not need that sort of conversation before going away?`

`I do. I must.` replied Sarah. She kissed Tony on the head and then Mark came over to the table.

`Come on darling, it's time for the first dance,` he held out his hands.

He smiled at Tony and swept Sarah onto the dance floor. David walked over and sat down next to his father. `She looks beautiful today and she's happy.`

`She is now. There was a time I didn't think this would ever happen,` replied Tony.

`What getting married?` enquired David curiously.

`Being happy,` replied Tony

`But she's strong,` said David.

`Is she,` replied Tony thoughtfully. `I'm not sure,`

`Yes, she's had to be and not just for herself,` said David. He looked at Tony and then they both turned and looked back at her dancing with Mark seemingly without a care in the world.

Chapter 16

It must have been late on a Friday evening towards the end of November in 1984 when the telephone rang in Tony and Carla's house. It was one of those awful Trimble phones, which produced a dialling tone that could only be compared to a cat purring with a whistle stuck in its throat. Carla was sat on the sofa watching the television holding a glass of vodka and orange to her lips, but not actually drinking it while Tony sat in a armchair reading the telegraph. The seeds of decay that had already quietly settled into bleak suburbia, but not yet begun to germinate, waited unwearyingly and patiently for the perfect environment in which to develop. One in which they might thrive exponentially, until the moment they became strong enough to accomplish their mission.

Tony put his paper down and looked at Carla to see whether she was going to lift the phone. She appeared to be totally engrossed in the program she was watching and seemingly unaware the phone was ringing despite it being much closer to her than him. He decided to get up and answer the phone rather than become involved in a pointless discussion over who should answer it. This was becoming a recurring and tiresome charade enacted out with frightening similarity to the third rate domestic soap drama in which she had become so absorbed.

Whenever the phone rang, Carla would feign deafness although anybody calling at that time of night invariably wanted to talk to her not him. Tony's friends seldom if ever rang during the evening for fear of encountering short shrift from Carla. They preferred to contact him during the course of the day at his place of work.

It was during the weekends and evenings when the children were now out on a more regular basis that he had begun to notice the change in their relationship. He couldn't pin down any specific moment when things began to change, neither could he isolate any one particular detail that may have instigated the deterioration, it had somehow just happened. Maybe, he thought, after what was now more than fifteen years, it was something that happened to every marriage. Maybe they all run out of steam, a spurious analogy at best, but one that somehow crudely, succinctly and rather neatly encapsulated the state of their relationship. The roaring passion and intensity of human spirit subrogated for a courteous almost respectful admiration, the rampant sexual chemistry now just a dutiful obligation. The recollections of voracious insatiable moments illicitly snatched on hot summer days in wild pastures and warm forbidden nights in tropical swimming pools all now reduced to fading specks of memory. The simple verity and integrity of which, even he had begun to doubt as they were constantly being withered and decimated by relentless time, the arrogant bedfellow and contumelious enemy of us all.

The children were all out - they seldom rang during the evening unless it was to say they would not be back until the following day and that was normally a call tactfully made much later in the evening when Tony would be less inclined to offer to pick them up.

`Hello,` said Tony in his polite if slightly starchy manner, `Tony Marshall.` Whenever answering the telephone his general timbre, inflection and accent would noticeably change to encompass a slightly if unintentional, uncharacteristic aristocratic twang, which belied his true heritage. If anything, this was the one mannerism, which had begun to irritate Carla, but she never mentioned it. Occasionally she winced with embarrassment, but not so he would notice. It seemed such an appallingly minor mannerism to give any credence to, but for some reason she did...

A drunken voice asked - `Is Sarah there?`

`No I'm sorry she's out at moment,` replied. Tony. He immediately recognised the voice.

'Where - is - she?' asked Malci in a staccato type delivery taking a deep breath at the end.

'I think she's gone round to her friend's house.'

'Who?' demanded Malci.

'I'm not sure,' replied Tony.

'Where's the house?' countered Malci, his tone becoming more aggressive.

'Warnsley Crescent,' replied Tony, trying not to rise to the harsh belligerence that was becoming evident in Malci's tone.

'What number?'

'I'm not sure to be honest. Do you want leave a message?'

Malci grunted something inaudible.

'She'll be back later,' Tony continued, he refused to be intimidated by Malci's manner and tried to maintain a calm and measured air of neutrality.

'Yea tell the fucking little bitch to get her arse round here or else.' He spluttered out.

'There's no need for that kind of language,' replied Tony in what was now a slightly more agitated tone. This attracted Carla's immediate attention. She was intrigued by the conversation Tony was having as it appeared to be more interesting than what she was watching on the television. 'I am trying to be as accommodating as I can despite your rude tones but,' he was interrupted....

'Look you fucking arse hole,' replied Malci, 'if I wanna fucking swear I'll fucking well will. I've 'ad your precious little slut of a daughter, fucked her up the arse, cunt and in 'er gob so don't put on all airs and graces with me mate cause I ain't fucking 'aving it you posh cunt.'

Tony didn't respond immediately while he digested Malci's diatribe.... 'I'll pass the message on,' replied Tony courteously refusing to be drawn in by Malci's drunken and abusive ranting.

`You do that you prickhead.`

`Is there anything else?` asked Tony politely, which was obviously only going to antagonise Malci further.

`No there fucking ain't,` he paused, `… cunt`

`Well goodnight then,` said Tony and he put the phone down.

`Was that Malci?` enquired Carla indifferently.

`Yes.` replied Tony sounding a little dazed, `I believe so.`

`Well was he upset or something,` asked Carla, `He sounded a bit loud from here.`

`A little!` replied Tony contemplatively, `he called me a cunt.` Tony repeated the word a couple of times with sanguine curiosity sounding almost as if he had never heard the word before and was endeavouring to search his memory for some long lost meaning.

Carla thought about it for a few seconds and decided it would be best just to ignore the comment and carry on with her conversation, which she did. `What did he want?`

`I not quite sure, but he said he wanted Sarah to go round as soon as possible.`

`Well she's out did you tell him that?`

`Yes, yes I did.`

`What else did he say?`

`He mentioned that he'd had sex with Sarah.`

`Did he?` replied Carla without any discernible emotion, which for some reason made him feel sick, `well lucky girl, least someone's getting some.`

Tony thought how sad it was, that that was all she had to say, but then maybe there was little else she could say. For some reason he was also deeply troubled by the revelation about the sex, he had always known that Sarah would eventually have her first sexual encounter with somebody, but had always imagined it would be with someone a little less despicable than the person he had just spoken to.

165

Although she was eighteen, as far as he was aware she had not had any other serious intimate relationships prior to Malci...

`Anything else?` continued Carla.

`No that was about it. Enough for me for one night anyway.`

`Why do you think she goes out with him?` asked Carla.

An interesting question thought Tony. `I've no idea. I presume she loves him.` It was a glib answer, almost a direct insult to her intelligence and it didn't even begin to explain the strange paradigm of their relationship, he knew that much and he didn't believe it for a moment. It was no answer at all in fact and Carla would undoubtedly punish him unmercifully for his indifferent, lackadaisical response. It was not slow in coming.

`Do you really believe that?` asked Carla, looking at Tony with an expression of crass naivety. She was lining up her ducks...

`I don't know what I believe anymore, only what I see and even that I'm not sure off. They sleep together and they appear to need each other, so there must be something there. Maybe that is love?

Ominously Carla stood up. `Do you love everybody you fuck?` she asked.

`What sort is question is that?` said Tony, realising immediately that this was a heavily loaded question requiring very careful consideration before he replied. Carla had developed the remarkable ability of being able to formulate surprisingly complex booby trapped questions cloaked in a deceivingly simple delivery, yet loaded with vitriol and bile. These could easily catch the unsuspecting recipient completely off balance.

`It was simple enough I thought. Well do you?` she persisted.

166

'It isn't simple at all. Firstly the question presupposes I have sex with someone else, whereas I don't, as you so nicely put it, fuck anybody else.'

'Well you don't fuck me, I know that much, so does that mean you don't love me?' asked Carla, who was now refilling her vodka and orange with more vodka.

'It doesn't mean that at all,' replied Tony defensively.

'Was does it mean then?' sniped Carla.

'It doesn't mean anything.'

'So I don't mean anything now,' said Carla, a clever misdirection thought Tony, a trick of verbal dexterity often used by Carla in an argument.

'No that's not what I meant,' replied Tony.

'So it does mean something?'

'You can love someone without having sex,' replied Tony.

'But Malci fucks Sarah, was does that mean. Do they love each other?' Carla said this in a stunningly naïve manner, it was as if they were two school children discussing the relationship of two friends.

'I don't know what it means,' replied Tony.

'Well I need to know, I need to understand.'

'Understand what?' said Tony.

'Why people make love, why they do it and we don't. Maybe you don't love me anymore that's why you don't fuck me.' Carla stared at Tony, engendering, demanding an answer.

'It's not me maybe it's you. Have you ever thought about that?' he replied.

'Me, nothing wrong with me,' said Carla indignantly.

'I didn't say there was anything wrong it's just that....'

'Just that what?' said Carla adopting a cynical expression.

'Sometimes you...'

167

`Here we go, you don't want sex so it's my fault, everything is always my fault, have you ever considered that maybe there might just be a chance that it's you and not me, maybe you just don't want to fuck me, that's it, plain and simple, you just don't fancy me anymore but you just haven't the guts to come out and say it.`

`You're right; I don't fancy you when you're like this.`

`Like fucking what?` cried Carla.

`Aggressive, argumentative, crude.`

`Crude, you didn't say that when I used to suck your dick.`

`I didn't mean it like that,` replied Tony.

`Well how did you mean it? you said crude not me. What would you like me to do wash, clean and iron your socks and be a good little girl? No more blowjobs for you, that's too crude.`

`I can't talk to you when you're like this.`

`Like what?` exclaimed Carla indignantly. `Sorry am I being too argumentative? Maybe you think it's a little too precocious of me having the temerity and audacity to think for myself, what with me being a woman who should really know her place.`

`I only said I wasn't sure what it was that Sarah and Malci had and that maybe it wasn't love, maybe it was something else, but whatever it is I don't understand it. I just wanted to know what you thought. I'm only her stepfather; you're supposed to know what's going on in her head.`

`She's a big girl, she can look after herself. Anyway, I don't want to talk about it. It's her problem not ours. It's her life so let her get on with it, she doesn't need our help to ruin it, I'm sure she can manage that all by herself.`

`But that's the whole point; I can't believe you just said that,` replied Tony, almost pleading with her. `She has a problem, her whole life seems to be disintegrating before our eyes and you just want to distance yourself from any involvement, isolate yourself from all the emotion and turmoil she is going through right now, which is precisely when we are supposed to be helping her, but you're just not interested.`

`If she has a problem, she's brought it on herself. So she's the best person to sort it out; we all have to suffer some pain in this life and much of it unfortunately on our own. So when some comes along and it's nothing to do with you, it's best left alone. As you said, I'm really not interested.`

`Has she ever hurt you? Did she do something to you that I don't know about?`

Carla thought about the question for a moment before answering, 'No.`

`Who hurt you then?` pleaded Tony.

`Nobody's hurt me.` replied Carla sitting back down on the edge of her chair, answering quietly.

`Was it me?` asked Tony.

`No not you,` replied Carla.

`Well somebody or something must have, to have made you this bitter, why won't you talk about it.` Tony looked at the woman he had once loved and wondered why it was that he no longer did.

`There's nothing to talk about, because nothing's hurt me, so unfortunately your pathetic attempt at schoolboy psycho analysis has taken you up the wrong garden path... again..` Carla was still on the defensive, but now in a less volatile way.

`Fair enough so why won't you help Sarah. That's what parents do. We're not supposed to become judgemental and hostile. We're supposed to help. That's what we're here for.`

`So I'm judgemental and hostile now, on top of argumentative, aggressive and oh crude, I'm not coming out of this very well am I?`

`I didn't say you were judgemental or hostile just that we shouldn't be, you are twisting my words.`

`Well you help her then,` said Carla.

`I will!` replied Tony quietly.

`Good!` Carla went a little quiet as well.

`Why do you dislike her so much?` asked Tony who was still very confused by Carla's attitude, it didn't seem to have any basis that he could understand.

`I don't dislike her. I told you I just don't want to talk about it OK.` Carla turned the television sound up and stared at the screen.

`Please don't do that, I want to talk about this.`

`Well I don't. If you want to talk about it why don't you go round to her friend's house and talk to her, maybe she will tell you all about it.` Carla sat back down in armchair.

`About what?` asked Tony curiously.

Carla hesitated for a moment. `Life!` Talk to her about life. You're very good at that.`

`Am I?` asked Tony, but Carla didn't answer.

Chapter 17

Harry now 13 years of age, quietly entered Sarah's, bedroom and carefully closed the door. The only illumination in the room from the nightlight at Sarah's bedside. Sarah was half-asleep, but quickly awoke when she heard the door close. She half turned over and looked at Harry still standing by the door. The expression, one of disarming coquettish and measured insouciance, seemingly way beyond her years. Harry smiled back with the naive innocence that besets some men to the grave. Sarah smiled without surprise, alarm, or desire, then turned back to face the other away. Tonight was no different from any other night as far back as she could remember. Without prompting she slowly removed her pyjama bottoms, pulled them out from beneath the bed clothes and tossed them nonchalantly over her shoulder to the floor. She glanced fleetingly back at Harry and in that moment encapsulated and polarised all the mesmerising particles of emotion that streamed between them. There was an ester of absolute purity in this entrapment something only discernible to and within the virginal parameters of the absolute honesty only experienced between siblings. Theirs was a love born out the natural affinity of a consanguineous relationship not because of it. Only in very rare circumstances does the familial liaison transcend to this level of affection. And then, only under exceptionally unusual conditions. It was as if they were the oxygen and nitrogen gases of the atmosphere haplessly coming together to form by absolute fortune, design or accident, the precise environment through which all other life would be allowed to exist.

She was not consciously aware of how or why she affected Harry this way, only that she did. This was pre-programmed, hardwired from birth. A Neanderthal defence mechanism. The woman stays at home and prepares it for her man, the hunter goes out into the world to bring home the food. She must please the hunter when he returns or she will not be fed.

Harry slipped off his pyjama bottoms and slid into bed close to Sarah.

'Do you love me?' asked Sarah softly. She knew what he would say, but she still needed to hear the words.

'Of course I do,' replied Harry. 'You are the only person I love, the only woman I will ever love.

Harry's use of the word "woman" thrilled her. She felt whole and complete; any feelings of doubt she may have harboured were now swiftly waved away. Her apprehension had increased over the last year and she was still unsure of exactly why she felt this way. She would mention these feelings from time to time to Harry but only to engender reassurances, which he always provided.

'But you're my brother Harry.'

'So!' replied Harry. Not fully understanding her question.

'You know it isn't right.' Sarah spoke not in a way that indicated objection, but more in a sense of innocent curiosity and inquisitiveness.

'You never said that before,' replied Harry sounding a little surprised.

'I never thought about it before.'

'Why are you thinking about it now?'

'I've been talking at school.'

'Who to?' enquired Harry, sounding a little alarmed.

'Friends, just friends,' replied Sarah.

'What did you say?'

'I just said I liked you.'

'That's alright I am your brother.'

'They thought it was a bit weird, liking my brother.'

'They're only jealous because we love each other,' replied Harry reassuringly.

'I don't think they know that,' said Sarah.

'No!' said Harry.

'Do we?' asked Sarah.

'Yes.'

'I don't think they do this,' said Sarah.

'How do you know? Did you ask them?' asked Harry a little arrogantly.

'No.'

'Then does it matter?'

'I don't know, I suppose not.'

Harry moved over on top of Sarah, and gently started to make love to her. No more the childish fumbling's of years ago, when they were learning about sex, now they made love as two people who knew each other's bodies intimately. They knew what to touch and what to caress and how to excite each other, but most all how to show each other that they cared, more for this than anything else on earth to the exclusion of all others.

'Nothing really matters now and in the end nothing matters at all?' said Harry sounding distant, as if there was something troubling his mind, for even now he had become resigned to the inevitable outcome that was drawing ever closer.

'Do you love me Harry?' asked Sarah again as Harry moved slowly up and down. 'I think I have always loved you.'

'We have always loved each other haven't we?' replied Harry gently kissing her neck.

'Yes we have, haven't we,' confirmed Sarah.

'Do I make you happy?' asked Harry.

'Yes, of course you do, you have always made me happy. You're the only person who has ever made me happy.'

173

`That's all I ever wanted to do you know,` replied Harry.

`I know,` said Sarah.

Sarah and Harry said nothing more. After they finished making love they began tenderly kissing for a few minutes, but there was a stilted awkwardness to it, which doused the last remains of the earlier sweet passion. Afterwards, they held each other very tightly for a while, as they lay in sweet surrender. From downstairs they could hear the muted strains of Dinah Washington singing `Since I fell for You.` on the music system. Tony and Carla were probably dancing. They often danced after they had argued.

`I wonder if mothers love all their children?` asked Sarah laying back on the bed gazing skywards. It was an odd question and Harry didn't answer straight away. There was obviously a hidden agenda in the context and he had become a little wary of such enquires.

`...Yes I think so,` replied Harry eventually.

`Why doesn't mummy love us then?` asked Sarah.

`I don't know,` replied Harry a little irritated and inwardly dismissive as he should have seen that coming. `Maybe that's what happens to everybody eventually.`

`Has she used it all up on David and Nigel - is that why there is none left for us?` It was a strangely innocent question but one that belied the obvious answer.

`Maybe,` replied Harry. `I don't really know anymore.` He sounded a little distant musing pensively over Sarah's words, but maybe she was right. He did know that he had drifted away from his parents long ago and even now he knew he was drifting away from Sarah. He was clinging to the wreckage at the moment, but for how much longer he wondered.

Chapter 18

It was a sunny Saturday morning, at the family home and Sarah had just arrived back for breakfast, but still dressed for the party she had been to the night before. She was still a little drunk as she indolently made her way into the kitchen where Tony, standing in his dressing gown was making a pot of tea. He turned and smiled a father's smile noticing the primal, slightly vacant air about Sarah that he had seen so many times before.

`Morning my little angel.` He always called her that first thing in the morning as far back as she could remember even though she was now nearly twenty one and far beyond the realms of angelic innocence. She could remember he used to bring a cup of tea and a chocolate biscuit up to all their rooms when she was six or seven. He did that every Sunday for years, but he had stopped doing it one day, for no particular reason as far as she aware and never did it again. She looked at his face as he made the tea and wondered if he was really happy. He had tried to accomplish so many things in his life, but they had all failed and now here he was nearly fifty and resigned to his life as a civil servant until he eventually retired, grew old and died. His overriding fear (although he seldom spoke of this) was that fifty years after his death he would be completely forgotten and no one would ever know he ever existed except as a name from the past. This was the way of the world, but as he grew older he became more concerned by the finality of existence and his nihilistic beliefs became more prevalent almost dominating his thoughts on occasions when he was either alone or sitting in his garden.

He had written books and all were rejected as being of no commercial worth despite him spending three or four hours a night for what must have been twenty years writing them. He tried oil painting for a few years but eventually gave that up in frustration never being able to ever accomplish a standard that could be honestly described by even his closest family or friends as anything more than a childishly naïve level of ability, which suffered badly from a basic lack of understanding and comprehension of the simplest fundamental concepts of perspective, proportion and balance. He persevered with trying to learn to play the piano (with the aid of a teacher) for nearly five years, but gave up one day when one of the neighbours children came in and played a flawless Clair de Lune and then apologised afterwards for playing the piece so badly or so she thought. Afterwards she explained that her parents couldn't afford piano lessons so she had to teach herself from listening to records and replicating what she had heard onto a primitive badly tuned upright that her parents kept in their garage. The tears started to roll down his face as he watched in stunned admiration as the child performed so easily what he then knew he would never master. He wanted so badly to do just one thing well and yet this was denied him despite all his efforts. He often wondered why it was that some people were so naturally gifted and yet wasted a talent when others who so desperately desired to achieve something of miniscule artistic merit never managed it. There was obviously some sort of astral-cosmic law, which strictly controlled the distribution of luck and talent, but he didn't know how it worked.

`Hi dad.` She leaned backwards against the door jamb just watching her father go through the simple routine of making the tea and wondering what she would be doing when she was his age. Tony wasn't exactly old, but his life had been mapped out for some time and was now unlikely to change very much before he retired. So in reality it was technically over as far as any radical career change were concerned.

`Cup of tea?` asked Tony. Sarah walked up behind her father and gave him a big hug.

`No thanks dad...I love you.` Impulsive acts of physical contact were much rarer these days and for that reason were always welcome and much appreciated. He often wondered whether as you grew older it became part of the closing ritual to slowly withdraw from tactile interaction. He and Carla seldom touched each other these days, it was something he missed.

`Love you too sweetheart,` responded Tony. `Did you have a nice night?` This was the general tone of most early morning chatter, irrelevant, inconsequential and nonspecific. It suited Sarah that Tony and Carla had ceased to ask searching questions each morning about her nocturnal activities.

`No not really, went to a club then back to a friend's house and decided to stay and have a drink as it was a bit late.` She rendered this explanation without coercion which was within the permitted unspoken parameters.

`Oh, Malci phoned!` Tony exclaimed as if he had momentarily forgotten the incident, which in fact he had.

`When?` replied Sarah, the atmosphere suddenly changing as she pulled away from Tony. The erratic, occasionally seismic charged moods swings were something he had never quite understood and never managed to predict with any degree of accuracy. The casual discernible nuance, a shaded inflection which would normally just float past him unnoticed or be simply ignored for its triviality and lack of gravitas, could transversely be interpreted by Sarah as something of such stupefying importance and sufficient relevance as to trigger or provoke alarm and personal anxiety out of all proportion to the intention or content.

`About eight. I told him you were at your friend's house. I thought he would know where that was.` Tony was surprised at her seemingly axiomatic over-reaction.

`Oh for Christ's sake, no. No he doesn't. I'll have to call him back.` Sarah immediately became very agitated about the missed call. The initially confident demeanour that she had so clearly demonstrated when entering the kitchen only a few moments earlier quickly evaporated, segueing into that of someone no longer at ease, someone who was now

177

becoming increasing restless and physically distressed. The acceleration of change even caught Tony by surprise. He had become conditioned to the regular hormonal variations in temperament, but this came from somewhere altogether different.

`I think he was drunk.` Tony quietly added as if it might assuage the situation.

`Was he?` she replied thoughtfully, but she appeared not to have clearly understood what Tony had said. Her mind was obviously miles away considering a myriad of possibilities and permutations.

`Why do you bother with him Sarah?  He's not a particularly nice person, you could do better.` An ill-timed observation, Tony thought afterwards. One that unfortunately was guaranteed to invoke an immediate defensive response.

`Have you been talking to mum about Malci?` replied Sarah firmly, but not overly abrasively for she had no quarrel with her father, but new full well his diffident reserved unobtrusive nature must have unintentionally absorbed some of Carla's less agreeable attributes with regards to her choice of boyfriend.

Tony subconsciously struggled against this unattractive morphing quality, but was perfectly aware that two people living together for any prolonged period of time would unfortunately - through no fault of their own - eventually suffer from a small degree of tacit synchronicity with regards to particular personal opinions. A situation probably brought about - with the passing years - by the acceptance of the necessity to compromise. Yes he thought to himself, the C word he despised most of all.

`A little,` said Tony, `why?`

`About what?` asked Sarah a little defensively.

`Well I had a telephone conversation with Malci that's all and Carla was listening.` Tony replied in a way which indicated it was of no consequence, but Sarah obviously thought otherwise.

`What did she say?` Sarah was becoming more agitated.

`Nothing much, just that she doesn't think he's right for you,` replied Tony. `But that's only her opinion I try not to....` he didn't finish, his expression said what he didn't.

`How would she know what's right for me?`

`She's just concerned for you...` said Tony calmly, in an effort to ease the growing tension, `...that's all.`

`Concerned for me, ha! Bit late for that,` replied Sarah bluntly. Tony presumed this was just normal juvenile feminine antagonism and didn't pursue the comment. But the reference lingered in his mind for a few days afterwards.

`I did wonder myself.` replied Tony with an inquisitorial intonation.

`He says he loves me and he needs me dad,` replied Sarah.

`I love you too, but I don't have to get drunk to tell you.`

`That's different dad,` replied Sarah.

`How's it different?` asked Tony.

`Parents love their children and protect them from everything and children love their parents because they are the first people they ever learn to love. They trust them explicitly without reservation before they become aware of the real world. This is the one and only definite in life. I don't trust religion. I don't trust morality and I don't believe there is any real reason for life, but I do believe in love when you find it and I have it with you and sort of with mum and,` she paused and went a little quieter, `...I have it with Malci. Maybe it won't last I don't know, but I have it for now and that's all that matters.` She lit a cigarette and walked towards the back door to open it.

`He wasn't particularly pleasant on the phone,` said Tony.

`What did he say?` asked Sarah rhetorically.

`He swore a lot and called me a few things.`

179

`He doesn't mean it. He can be really nice when he's not drunk,` said Sarah apologetically.

`So there are days when he's....` but Sarah interrupted before he could finish

`Yes Dad, there are and I'm sorry he swore at you but...`

`You don't have to apologise for him he can do that himself. I just don't understand what you see in him.`

`I told you dad. He needs me and I need him. I have to have someone to love me, someone whose is mine.` Tony looked at the tormented face of his daughter, no longer a girl, but a woman visibly tearing her heart out and throwing it to the hungry wolves to keep them at bay. Someone he loved dearly crying out for something he couldn't give her. This made him feel as wretched as hell. He thought about her words and wondered if everybody had this desire, he had never felt it with Carla, but then she was completely self-contained and generated her own confidence, her own defence mechanism. In reality he had never felt it with anybody and thought that maybe that said more about him than other people.

`Does he or is he just using you?`

`We all use each other at one time or another,` replied Sara cynically.

`Is that what you think?` replied Tony a little surprised at her uncharacteristically disparaging analysis, `sounds very cynical for you.`

`Does it? You need mum to cook and wash and clean and for sex. She needs you to bring the money home to pay the bills. We need you to feed us. Your company needs you to make money for them and they need customers to make money for them to pay you so you can feed us and we all take advantage of the arrangement. The very system that exists for our very survival and yet we all inwardly despise it and we abuse it. We're all users - users and abusers.` Tony smiled at the pure simplistic, if somewhat naïve assessment, but found it strangely uncomfortable. It was too near the

180

truth, Sarah had delivered a compelling argument and there was little he could say to refute it. He was also a little disturbed by the savagery of the underlying implications of the sexual comment, a subtle agenda that made him feel very uneasy with himself.

`But why do you need him?` asked Tony warily.

`Dad nobody else ever loved me accept you, and you have her... I want somebody of my own. That is why I need him.`

`Your mother loves you too.`

`She doesn't really love me, she has never loved me. I sometimes wonder if she even knew the meaning of the word.`

`You don't mean that, she brought you into the world, she gave you life and looked after you since the day you were born that's what love is really all about.`

`She may have given me life, but she also took it away,` replied Sarah with an unsettling murmur.

`What do you mean took it away?` asked Tony, `What does that mean? She has always been there for you whenever you wanted her.` The unusual phrase fired with uncharacteristic vitriol had rattled him a little, it seemed to find its mark.

`No she hasn't dad, not really there for me and she's not there for you either.` There was a sense of recalcitrant banality entwined within the veiled gentility of her voice that effused flickering doubts into a part of his soul he had not visited for a long time. Her lambent ability to touch and invade that sacrosanct area with such solicitous ease did nothing to dissuade his gravest fears.

`You don't really believe that,` replied Tony defensively, a little surprised at the assertion.

`Yes I do dad, do you want me to lie to you?`

`No. No I don't want you to lie to me, What I need to understand is why you feel this way.`

`Do you really want to know how I feel,' she paused for a few moments to gaze at Tony her eyes peering deep into his soul, 'I feel dirty dad, that's what I am and that's how I feel, messed up, dirty, empty and worthless.` Sarah started to cry.

`Hey what's brought this on?` Tony was taken off guard by this sudden outcry as he had obviously misjudged the situation. While he thought he was simply dealing with the machinations of her relationship with Malci, he now realised he had become inveigled into something much deeper, something that went way beyond his peripheral comprehension of current events. He pulled Sarah close to cuddle her, but she instinctively pulled away.

`Dad, I've never told anyone what I really feel like, every moment of every day, when I get up in the morning, when I go to bed, when I'm drunk and when I'm sober... I always feel the same, worthless that's what I'm feeling right now utterly completely worthless.`

`Hey come on now princess don't be silly.` whispered Tony trying to comfort her and pulling her back toward him, but suddenly feeling completely inadequate.

`I count for nothing; nobody really wants me or loves me except for you, dad. Do you know all I've ever wanted is for someone to love me, someone to hold me, just to make me feel good inside. That's not asking too much is it.'

`No, that's not. That's what we're all looking for.`

`Really? What even you?` asked Sarah sounding a little surprised.

`We all need that reassurance, no matter what anybody might tell you.`

`Malci says he loves me and do you know what, that actually makes me feel good. That piece of slimy drunken dog shit actually makes me feel good about myself. I know deep down he probably doesn't really love me and I know he's probably only using me, but if this is as good as it gets and its make me feel a little better, then I'll take it, every bit of it, 'cause that's all that's going.`

`Why does he treat you like that?`

`I don't know, maybe he knows me better than I know myself, maybe he understands how I feel. He may even feel the same, I don't know, kindred spirits and all that I don't know, but do you know what, I don't care all I know is he wants me. Every day he wants me and I'll do anything absolutely anything just to hang onto that feeling.` Sarah wiped her eyes. `Just to know that one person wants me so badly that they will do anything for me. Me! dirty, worthless useless ugly me, that's what he wants me, me, ... I know I'm at the bottom of a sewer swimming around in the shit, but I just don't care... My mother hates me, do you know that I actually think she hates me. I can't ever remember her giving me a cuddle not once, not once in my whole life.` She looked up at Tony for some sort of reaction. ` I bet you can't ever remember seeing her do that can you?`

`...She must of...` stuttered Tony, not with the instantaneous spontaneity of an honest response - one without a second thought - without the necessity for consideration or reflection, without a moment of doubt or unencumbered by reservation, but one shamefully slow, maybe only by the smallest fraction of a mini second in time, but still delayed enough to make all the difference in the world to the veracity and integrity of the answer. The brain makes remarkable assumptions based on nothing more than what happens in a split second. More often than not, the assumption is correct. It has an inert ability to interpret the nuance, the facial expression, the body language, the colour of your cheeks and so many other things that combine so perfectly to steal the credence of verity.

The delay in replying with immediacy was in itself a condemnation, as he was finding it very hard to deny the damming accusation. `I don't remember a specific occasion,` he stuttered on, `but then you don't remember things like that, they're a bit like breathing. It happens all the time but you don't notice it or think about.` Tony was almost apologising for what appeared to be an accusation of a lifetime of not noticing something so fundamental, but as he was about to earn he too had missed many things.

Sarah felt embarrassed for him she knew he was just an innocent bystander caught up in the crossfire. `I do.` she said. `I remember every little detail of my childhood. She always cuddled David and Nigel, but she never held me because she hated me; she blames me for everything that went wrong. `Sarah walked back towards the door and turned to face Tony. `It wasn't his fault he wasn't to blame not her precious little Harry it was me, always me, always my fault I was to blame. So fair enough, what do I care? I'll find someone one day somebody who will really love me and hold me then I'll be happy, but for now I'll take Malci because he wants me.`

`I've always loved you. You know that.` said Tony, but he was confused and couldn't understand what Sarah was alluding to.

`I know you have dad. But mummy should have loved me too, she had no right to...` Tony moved across the kitchen to hug her again, tears welled up in both their eyes.`

`Don't tell mummy will you?` begged Sarah, `about this.`

`There's nothing to tell,` replied Tony reassuring her again.

`It's our secret isn't it,` said Sarah unnervingly childlike.

`Our secret,` confirmed Tony smiling. Suddenly Sarah pulled away from Tony.

`We only did it because we were lonely. She never loved us; we had to look after each other. He said he loved me and I was lonely. We were both lonely.` There was an element of confusion in this declaration which Tony still couldn't make sense of.

`What you do with Malci is your business, no one else's and if he makes you happy then...` Sarah stopped him, by putting her finger to his lips and shut her eyes.

`No Dad,` she said quietly with a vestige of apprehension that was almost indiscernible `Not Malci...` she paused,

184

opened her eyes and looked directly at Tony. `Harry, me and Harry when we were young, that's the secret.`

`What did you do pinch biscuits from the kitchen and have a midnight party?` replied Tony with a disarming smile.

`No dad, we used to cuddle up in bed together when we were little. Harry used to love me, we loved each other, because mum didn't.`

`Well That's OK there's nothing wrong with that, brothers and sisters always do that.`

`Harry made love to me dad.` Tony heard what she said, but it just refused to enter his brain and seemed to hang in the air. There was something not quite right about it and he needed to get it right before allowing the words to pass into his brain to be processed for eternity into memory bank.

`Sitting it bed together isn't making love darling you know that.` said Tony innocently still trying to explain away what she was saying.

`No dad, Harry made love to me...` There was a moments silence while Tony absorbed the words, but he was still having a problem with the ambiguity.

`Made love, no... ` he replied `You were having a cuddle and eating biscuits under the sheets. That is different that is not making love darling, that's OK. You were what four or five? and Harry would have been seven or eight that is not bad. Brothers and sisters all do that when they're young..

`No dad,` she paused, `we made love, we had sex, he entered my body dad, he fucked me..... for over ten years he fucked me dad, almost every night he fucked me...now do you understand.....`

Chapter 19

Harry was sitting up in his bed slowly and intensely twirling a pencil in his hand and gazing out of his window at some indeterminate point in the distance while listening to Keane playing "Can't stop now" on his headphones.

Sarah knocked gently on Harry's door and cautiously entered his room. She was wearing her wedding dress, which surprised and slightly confused Harry. Her pervasive presence in the room engendered a heavy exquisite languor, which somehow seemed to envelope the whole room and consume all the available oxygen. For a moment, Harry could not breathe. A less ethereal entrance than that of Doris earlier that day, but nevertheless, blindingly mesmerising and for the remainder of his lifetime unforgettable.

`What are you doing here? Aren't you supposed to be getting married today?` asked Harry with an oddly vicarious inflection. His head were now cast downwards towards his hands as if in an act of supplication. He spoke as if he were addressing himself and only fleetingly glimpsed up at her through the top of his eyes. He thought if he did not see her, it might not be true.

`I am Harry, in a couple of hours,` replied Sarah.

`Then why are you here you should be with him and all your friends and the people you love today.`

`I needed to know something,` replied Sarah.

`Must be important to leave your wedding?` Harry lifted his head slightly still looking at Sarah through the top of his eyes, not prepared to look directly at her.

`They won't miss me for half an hour, Mark will tell them something.`

`He knows you're here?` exclaimed Harry with a tiny cadence of visceral concern in his voice.

'Yes,` replied Sarah choosing not to deny the assumption, 'of course.` He didn't and Sarah wondered why she had spontaneously decided to lie to Harry over something so trivial.

'You could have come tomorrow, you didn't have to.. ` Sarah put a finger to his lips.

'I had to come today, I had to make sure you were OK.`

'I'm fine,` replied Harry smiling briefly.

'You don't look fine,` replied Sarah, dismissively casting her eyes around the room.

'I had an accident...`

'Did you?` asked Sarah with an expression that implied total disbelief. The words seemed to hang in the air.

'I will miss you,` said Harry.

'You can visit us, we won't be living that far away.`

'I don't want to visit you and see you playing happy families,` replied Harry. He gazed expressionlessly at Sarah.

'I can't visit you,` said Sarah. There was a finality in her words that reached deep down into his soul.

'Why not?` replied Harry with a benign naivety, that belied the reality of their situation

'You know why not,` replied Sarah.

'But what am I supposed to do? I don't want anybody else.`

'Harry it's nearly twenty years since you left home, we've hardly mentioned it over the last ten years, so why this and why now?`

'I can't forget what happened, what passed between us. I don't want to forget. I want what we had. I don't want anything else. You belong to me.`

'We can never be together again, that was all over long ago, it should never have happened I got over it, I thought you had,` replied Sarah sternly rebuking Harry for his posturing.

187

`Does he make you happy?` asked harry after a few moments absorbing what she had just said.

`Yes. He loves me and that makes me happy, very happy,` said Sarah.

`Like I made you happy, when we loved each other.`

`I loved you once, but not now. That has ended.

`But why?` asked Harry with a frisson of desperation that Sarah could feel in a place she had almost forgotten existed.

`It's different now, it was different then.` Sarah tried to avoid direct eye contact for a second. She wasn't sure she could hold out.

`Do you love him?` asked Harry. It was a mournful plea, almost a cry of desperation but then that's what it really was. If necessary, he would test her resolve to the point of destruction.

`I told you, it's different.`

`So you're deceiving him,` asked Harry, relentlessly probing for a weakness in her protective shell.

`No,` replied Sarah, `I am not deceiving him.`

`Does he know?` Harry asked slowly and deliberately.

`Know what?` replied Sarah.

`About us, about real love.`

`That's a trick question,` replied Sarah.

`There are no trick questions, just questions.`

`Yes there are and I won't answer it,` replied Sarah

`That's up to you,` said Harry smiling.

`That's right,` said Sarah belligerently. `It's up to me.`

Harry watched Sarah as she began to walk around the room looking at the pictures, purposely avoiding direct eye contact.

`But you're fooling yourself, It's like a seduction you know?`

`What is?` asked Sarah.

188

`Deception is like a seduction, didn't you know that.`

`I don't know what you are talking about.`

`For deception to exist one party must be willing to consent to overlook certain inconsistencies in a routine. Clues if you like that would, to an open mind, unfazed and unclouded by the intimacies and fantasies of passion, become glaring obvious evidence of an infidelity.`

`And where is this going?` asked Sarah feigning boredom, but listening intently to what Harry was saying.

`Please let me continue,` replied Harry. `The deceived subconsciously blocks outs anything that can destroy the deception, because the deceived actually wants the illusion to continue. Either that or he or she, whatever the case is, risks losing everything and...`

`Theatrical fantasy,` interjected Sarah.

`Fantasy, illusion, whatever, but you see the seducer or deceiver cannot be entirely to blame when he has a willing accomplice who by the very act of deceit is a party to what transpires.`

`And what does that mean?` said Sarah.

`He must know.`

`He does not,` Sarah firmly confirmed.

`You haven't told him?`

`No why should I?`

`Why shouldn't you?` replied Harry

`Because.....` Sarah didn't finish

`So you've deceived him already?`

`Ah you think you're so clever,` said Sarah.

`No I'm not clever I'm just trying to decide who is what in this ménage a trios,` replied Harry.

`There is no ménage a trois as you so nicely put it, there's just Mark and me,` replied Sarah

`And me,` added Harry.

`You're not part of us we are a perfect couple.`

`Are you?` replied Harry, `but you've deceived him and he's deceived you.`

`Mark hasn't been unfaithful.`

`I didn't say that, I said he's deceived you.`

`How?`

`He must know about us, but he's not saying anything so he's deceiving you,` said Harry.

`You've told him!` exclaimed Sarah.

`No I haven't but deep down he knows or he will know.`

`How?`

`You'll say something, something very small, insignificant, but it will be the first small seed of doubt. But his love for you will blind him to the truth and he will ignore it, because he won't want to believe it and that belief will be stronger than his curiosity, but that's when he starts to deceive you.`

`We'll see.`

`Will you have children?` asked Harry.

`Probably.`

`Will you love them no matter what happens?`

`Yes, you know I will.`

`Will you protect them?`

`Off course?`

`But will you know?`

`Know what?`

`Whether it has started again?`

Sarah looked directly at Harry... `It won't.`

Then it's not all been for nothing?` replied Harry

`No I don't think so.`

`Do you regret anything? asked Harry

`Like what?`

`Loving me,` said Harry.

`Was that what it was?` asked Sarah still wandering around the room gazing intently at the few pictures, any distraction to avoid looking at Harry.

`So do you?` repeated Harry

`Do I regret loving you?

`Yes.` said Harry

`No. No I don't. You saved me Harry. I was drowning and you saved me and I'm happy now, so no I don't regret it, not any part of it, but it's over now.`

`I'm glad,` whispered Harry. He seemed more relaxed, more at ease now that Sarah had been honest with him. This maybe was all he really wanted to hear.

`For what?`

`Well I don't feel quite so bad about it now,` said Harry

Sarah smiled, `I must get back.`

`Yes you must, they might think you've had a change of heart.`

`Bit late now,` said Sarah waving her wedding ring at Harry, `I love you Harry.`

`Love you to Sarah, goodbye.`

Sarah moved back towards the bed and kissed Harry on the forehead.

`See you soon,` said Harry.

`See you soon Harry,` repeated Sarah. She closed the door behind her.

Chapter 20

Tony and Sarah cont…

Tony is lost for words as he goes over in his mind what Sarah has just told him.

`You mean...`

`He fucked me dad and it didn't stop for nearly ten years, until I was fifteen, till Harry left home. We made love; we had sex for nearly ten years.

`Sex but you couldn't you were only....`

`Five I was only five when it started, that's right.`

`You were just messing around, all brother and sisters mess around when they're young it couldn't . . .`

`He played with me at the beginning dad and then it turned to sex. I let him. He said he loved me.`

`But you couldn't have done it for.. ` Tony was still struggling to come to terms with the time line and their ages.

`Ten years dad all of my childhood. That's why I'm so messed up.`

`That's not possible, that couldn't have happened, I am not doubting what you say, but you must be confused. Your mother would have known something was going on and she. . `

Sarah interrupted. `She did dad. I told her time and time again, but she wouldn't do anything so I stopped telling her? She wasn't interested in me, she didn't care. She said I must have been making it up. Then when she realised I wasn't, she said it was my fault because I was promiscuous and I must have led him on. Eight years old and bloody promiscuous. I didn't even know what the word meant until I was eleven and by then Harry had been raping me for nearly seven years and still it didn't stop.`

`I tried to speak to her again when my periods started, but she just closed me out. She told me not to be stupid and not to say anything to you or you wouldn't love me anymore, I think she was even jealous that you loved me.`

`How come I never knew what was going on? Why didn't you speak to me?`

`Dad ... I know you're my dad but, you're not my real father and you're not Harry's dad you just married our mum. How could you expect me to come to you, a stranger at the beginning and tell you what was happening when my real mum didn't believe me? By the time I thought I could tell you it was too late, it had been going on too long. And then Harry left home and it stopped and I thought it was over.`

`But you could have told me, I would have listened I could have done something.`

`Dad, if I told you, you would have hated me, you would have hated us both. Mum already hated me, I didn't want to lose you as well.`

`Don't be silly, I love you both. Nothing would have changed that.`

`Not even this? Don't be silly dad. It would have ripped the family apart. I was already hurting. There was no need for anyone else to know. What good would that have done?`

`It would have stopped.`

`Maybe, but after a while I wasn't so sure I wanted it to stop anymore. Anyway it's all dirty water down the plughole now.` She smiled disarmingly at her odd metaphor.

`What about Harry?`

`What about him?` said Sarah.

`Was he ever going to tell me?`

`We were both going to tell you a few years ago and then... well he couldn't do it...`

`That's when he took the first overdose!` exclaimed Tony with sudden realisation.

`Yes. After that I promised him I would never tell you and he promised he wouldn't do it again, but he can't deal with this any better than I can. You have no idea how he feels. I still don't know how he really feels when he talks to me.`

`What you still talk about it?`

`We used to. He did promise one day he would come and talk to you about it, to try and sort it out but.. `

`What have we done to you both?`

`You've done nothing, everybody did nothing, everybody does nothing. Isn't that how bad things happen. You're not to blame for any of this; you're just a bystander on the sidelines. It all started long before you even arrived.`

`But you were three when I met your mum.`

`If Harry ever does talk to you he'll say it all started when he was only three and I wasn't even born?`

`What started?`

`I can't tell you that, you will have to ask mummy or Harry it's nothing to do with me.`

`She will never tell me.`

`Then speak to Harry he might.`

`I'm so sorry for what has happened and I will help put it right. I will speak to your mother.`

`No please don't dad. Promise you won't tell her I told you, it won't make any difference now. I actually sort of get on with her now and I don't want to lose that. Promise me, please?`

`Is that what you really want?`

`Yes dad.`

`That's a heavy promise.`

`Thank you dad and don't worry I will move on and maybe even get shot of Malci one day.`

Tony smiled. `Well that's something I suppose.`

`I love you dad.`

`I love you to darling.` Tony cuddled Sarah and then she picked up her mobile phone to make a call...

Chapter 21

The wedding reception had been going on since early afternoon and Sarah and Mark decided it was a good time for them to slip away while everybody was still having a good time and before the "finger munching started" as Mark so delicately put it. He had been to quite a few weddings over the past few years, mainly friends from the rugby club and in his considerable experience, invariably at some point during the evening it would develop an unpleasant dimension. It would be the time when a few of the guests, the ones who had let the alcohol get the better of them, decided to trade a few insults and punches and settle old scores.

On this occasion discretion being the better part of valour he thought it best to leave before proceedings got underway. A strong Scottish contingency unfortunately predominantly from his side of the family would undoubtedly find fault with the "Southern pansies" and seek some sort of final retribution for Culloden.

`I suppose you're going?` asked Tony sounding a little disappointed.

`We thought we would slip away now. Mark is just ringing the taxi company, is that OK dad?`

`Of course it is they're all drunk anyway.` replied Tony.

`Are you sure dad?`

`Yes of course I am, it's whatever makes you happy now that's all that matters.' Tony paused for a moment, 'You are happy now aren't you?`

`Of course I am it's been a lovely day, we can't thank you enough and I'm really happy.`

`With everything?` Tony asked looking at her searchingly, but she didn't answer straight away and he couldn't read her face anymore not like he used to be able to. All he could see now was the gravitational pull of a new energy source emanating from her soul sucking in the strength and determination and confidence from all around and expunging the timidity and helplessness and lack of self-esteem that had plagued her for a lifetime.

`I went to see him today.` she said quietly.

Tony knew instinctively to whom she was referring. `What did he say?` asked Tony.

`He asked me if I was still happy as well...`

Chapter 22

Harry was now eighteen and Sarah fifteen when he entered her bedroom for the last time to commence a routine that had continued for so long she had now almost forgotten when it started. She sat up in bed and looked at him and smiled. She lifted the top of her pyjamas to reveal the breasts that he had watched develop over the years and that he had held so many times. He was still fascinated by her wilfulness.

`Are you getting in?` she whispered rhetorically and without hesitation he slipped into the bed alongside her. They turned to face each other and smiled before gently embracing. The harsh fumbling clumsiness and naivety of early years when they were teaching each other what their bodies could do was now replaced by a mutual understanding of what they both desired. Gentle fingers stroked and caressed every inch of their bodies, arousing them slowly with an intensity that was physically painful to contain, before they started kissing passionately, then making love with an irrational abandonment of everything not connected to what they doing. Throughout the whole time, they were almost completely silent their mouths screamed out words of encouragement, but without making a sound. For not an utterance could be permitted. Sometimes they would bite each other so hard that at the moment of orgasm that they would draw blood from each other. But better the pain than recrimination on discovery. One night he asked her in a whisper just before they climaxed whether she was happy. She considered the question as carefully as she could, but now devoid of all natural emotion having been ritually raped for so many years she was unable to differentiate between right and wrong. She had become amoral and would now cling desperately to any form of relationship in the hope of finding love even though she was not sure exactly what that was. She reacted without accountability and in her search for reason she instinctively replied.

`Do you want me to be?`

`Yes of course I do.` replied Harry

`Then I'm happy,` said Sarah. They continued making love moving slowly toward the final climax…

~~

…Sarah stood outside the reception gazing across the green while still talking to Tony. The DJ was playing Keane's "The last Time."

`And what did you say?` asked Tony.

`I told him I was,` replied Sarah, then she turned to Tony and asked him `Do you want me to be happy?` Tony thought it was an odd question to ask.

`Of course I do darling, that's all that ever matters.` He smiled, `I'll go and tell everybody you are leaving.  You will have to do the confetti bit again unfortunately…` Sarah smiled and Tony started to walk back in and then turned back and looked at Sarah and asked,

`Are you happy?` he asked, Sarah didn't answer…

Chapter 23

A smoky nightclub in old Havana.

To the hypnotically passionate strains of Por Una Cabeza being played out by an old Cuban guitarist and a beautiful violinist, I could see Harry moving with an intensity I had not seen before. As they danced Harry spoke to his partner..

`Are you happy darling?`

`Do you want me to be?` she casually replies.

`Of course I do that is all I have ever wanted.`

As they slowly turn into the light, Sarah stops for a moment and smiles at Harry.

`Then I am happy. I will always love you and I will always be happy.` They carry on dancing...

~~

It was late evening back at the hospital on the wedding day and Harry was playing the same music on his IPOD. He rhythmically tapped out the infectious Latin rhythm with a pencil on the side of his face and then he scratched his nose with the pencil.

He turned to look out of the window, out across the green to the church spire that he could just see in the distance and then slowly, but firmly slid the first four inches of the pencil into his nostril until he felt some token resistance. He changed hands so that he was holding the pencil with his left hand and quite deliberately without any hesitation gave one swift punch with the heal of his right hand which propelled the pencil through his nasal membrane bursting into the lower cortex of the frontal lobe of his brain, almost without making a sound. He lurched just for a second and his body became momentarily rigid as the trauma initially resisted the message, but then the shock registered into his central nervous system and he gracefully sank back onto the pillow. His eyes slowly closing as the blood began to trickle down his nose and drip off the end of the pencil falling onto the bed sheet. His arms fell away onto the bed and his head fell back onto the pillow. The song that he was listening to stopped playing as if cued to end at that precise moment.

In the few seconds before he died he suddenly remembered his bedroom back in 1981 when they had just arrived, after nearly an hour of sybarite but passionate foreplay, at the moment when their bodies shuddered together erotically in a moment of divine consummate pleasure, the like of which they were both unlikely to ever experience again with such intensity.

At the reception Mark was standing outside saying goodbye and Sarah was just getting into the car when she turned to Tony who was throwing confetti along with the other guests and looking at him she smiling...

`Dad!` she shouted from the car.

`Yes darling,` Tony shouted back.

`That question you asked me?`

`Yes?` replied Tony

`The answer is yes, yes I am.  But then  I always have been.`

The car drove away leaving Tony standing alone with his thoughts and wondering.

THE END

Epilogue

'This world is all nonsense. How long must I endure it?'
{Morgan Le Fay. le Morte d'Arthur] Thomas Mallory.

Before you begin any journey, there is always a decision to be made.   You must be prepared to except the consequences of that decision whatever they are. To read a book is a journey, from which you will return as someone who may have changed, maybe only slightly,   almost imperceptibly even to those who know you intimately, but never the less there will be a change from the way you were before you began the journey. A book can inspire you to do those things you have not done, but should have; or transport you to places where you thought you would never go, or conjugate disparate thoughts about things you never dared think about before.

The decision you have to make - before the inevitable onset of cerebral deterioration due either to the passing of the of years, or the excessive consumption of alcohol or other chemicals - in order to, with some reasonable degree of integrity and alacrity, accurately recall the factual and chronological order of events and also to retain some degree of detachment, is:

Should the writer, before embarking on this voyage of discovery either,

(1) Adopt the simple guise of an Edward Hopper voyeur: making no contact and taking only contemporaneous notes, whilst carefully evaluating the events as they unfold, with a strict nonpareil impartiality. Or

(2) The position of casually acquainted observer with limited by-partisan interest in the initial proceedings but enfranchised to make minor comments and suggestions: or

(3) Become an active participant ultimately someone who would by his very connection with and integration into the events, become intrinsically involved with the protagonists.

The latter option would be his choice. This, despite a level of deterioration in his ability to accurately recall the events, which would, paradoxically be equivalent to his expanding comprehension of the fundamental finely balanced nature of the events, which were to follow.

Inexorable depths of the soul, even into the darkness of hell must first be plunged before you can see the light. If you find yourself travelling through purgatory, keep travelling. Therefore, a sense of propriety is essential as you approach the closing days of your life. If, at some future date, an appraisal of the subject matter were to be undertaken, then reference to this story with any degree of objectivity integrity and impartiality could be seriously impeded if the writer were to adopt the position of active participant. Someone who could be materially and emotionally affected by the events and therefore inclined, possibly unintentionally over a period of time, to refine rearrange, alter, modify or even completely rewrite the chronological order and contextual arrangement to better suit their overall recollection of events and personal raison d'être.

The primary motivation for reviewing past events is to determine, whether the original conclusions were fundamentally correct and if so could those decisions form a structural platform from which the outcome of a future issue could be determined. The options are thus reduced to two:

Should I espouse the role of voyeur, someone without any knowledge of the proceedings and therefore exposed to the possibility of misinterpretation of events due to the lack of sufficient detailed and relevant pertinent information.

Or, casually acquainted observer with the primeval imagery and visceral latitude in his experience of life in general and of these events in particular and the answer I believe is the latter. This is the least subjective position to adopt having first embraced and then discarded the misconception that distance and time lends an element of enchantment be it a slightly foggy interpretation over the central argument.

So there we have it, the decision is made and I begin… and continue to dream for in this, I am at ease with the day and I fear not starvation for the dream will satiate my hunger. I fear not death for I am already dying and with this triviality, I have already come to terms and I fear not losing for all is now lost…..and therefore, I no longer fear the truth for this will set me free.

There is innocence in pain. The purity, the unblemished reality that nothing can take away the hurt. Absolute pain is unhindered and unimpeded by guilt, reason, or accountability. It takes everything and gives nothing in return. It should be embraced for what it is. It stands alone as the one true dependable experience. It needs no purpose for it polarises the mind and in doing so permits the recipient, the transcendental ability to focus exclusively on what is happening at that moment. All other metaphysical senses have a vague, pointless rational and are in constant battle for control. Love, hate, beauty, sexual gratification, are shallow, fleeting and self-serving, whereas pain plunges deep into the body and caresses the soul. We must accept responsibility for our deeds, even if only guilty of impassioned ignorance and naivety. The fragility of our very existence depends on whether we are prepared to accept this. We learn from experience and if we do not learn from the past then we are destined to repeat our mistakes in the future. Some say the past is no indication of what we can expect in the future, but this is a contradiction, because it defines conversely something that cannot be defined and the statement is therefore dependent on the contradiction. If the past is no indication of the future than the past may or may not replicate itself, but the future will always be whatever we make it. This is a recollection of the events surrounding the life and death of Harry.

Some say the past is no indication of what we can expect in the future, but this is a contradiction, because it defines conversely something that cannot be defined and the statement is therefore dependent on the contradiction. If the past is no indication of the future than the past may or may not replicate itself, but the future will always be whatever we make it. This is a recollection of the events surrounding the life and death of Harry.

30551517R00117

Made in the USA
Charleston, SC
19 June 2014